THE COLOR ATLAS
OF HUMAN ANATOMY

Edited by Vanio Vannini and Giuliano Pogliani

Translated and revised by
Dr. Richard T. Jolly, M.B., B.S., M.R.C.S., L.R.C.P. (London)

BEEKMAN HOUSE

NEW YORK

PUBLISHER'S NOTE

This is not a medical text but a general introduction for the layman which presents the human body graphically and dramatically. It should serve to stimulate the reader's curiosity and lead him to further study and exploration.

Originally published in 1979 as
Nuovo Atlante Del Corpo Umano
Edited by Vanio Vannini and Giuliano Pogliani
by Gruppo Editoriale Fabbri S.p.A., Milan, Italy.

Copyright © on the series "Biblioteca medica" 1979 Gruppo Editoriale Fabbri S.p.A., Milano © on the volume "Nuovo atlante del corpo umano" 1979 Gruppo Editoriale Fabbri S.p.A., Milano - first edition in "Il dizionario della medicina © 1978 Gruppo Editoriale Fabbri S.p.A., Milano.

Translation and revision copyright © 1980 by Dr. Richard T. Jolly.

This edition is published by Beekman House,
a division of Crown Publishers, Inc.,
by arrangement with Gruppo Editoriale Fabbri S.p.A., Milano.

g h

BEEKMAN 1980 EDITION

This book is set in Photon Times.

Made and printed in Italy by Gruppo Editoriale Fabbri S.p.A., Milano

Library of Congress Cataloging in Publication Data

Main entry under title:

The Color atlas of human anatomy.

"Originally published as Nuovo atlante del corpo umano."
Includes index.
1. Anatomy, Human—Atlases. I. Vannini, Vanio. II. Pogliani, Giuliano. III. Jolly, Richard T. (DNLM: 1. Anatomy—Atlases. QS17 N973)
QM25.C64   611   80-68640
ISBN 0-517-31934-9

Contents

INTRODUCTION

Human curiosity, when turned on the self, has taken many forms – anthropology, psychology, the writing of biography, for example. Perhaps the most telling of such explorations is the examination of the human form, which constitutes the study of anatomy.

In the line of artists, doctors, and teachers who have refined or revolutionized the science of human anatomy, Leonardo da Vinci (1452–1519) led the way. That most eminent and gifted Renaissance man was certainly a revolutionary, with his drawings, accomplished from dissections, of the principal bones and muscles of the body and with his analytic studies of the eye. Of course, Leonardo was fascinated as much by the way things worked as he was by how they

looked. He constructed and experimented with models to demonstrate how bodily systems functioned.

His successor in the field of scientific anatomy was Andreas Vesalius. At age 29 in 1543, Vesalius published his seven-volume *De humani corporis fabrica (On the Fabric of the Human Body)*. As Leonardo had, Vesalius worked from actual anatomical dissection. He drew beautiful large, detailed anatomical charts, showing bones and muscles as they looked in motion. He used these to teach his students at Padua, Italy. In his *Fabrica*, he carefully integrated text and drawings. Students and professors immediately realized the worth of Vesalius' drawings, which were widely copied. Vesalius himself, a battlefield surgeon as well as a great teacher, was greatly in demand as a physician to European princes.

In the centuries since Vesalius, medical knowledge of human anatomy has expanded enormously and books have dramatically chronicled this knowledge. Among the major scientists making new discoveries was William Harvey (1578–1657), lecturer on anatomy and physician to James I and Charles I of England. Harvey had studied at Padua, a mere generation or so after Vesalius had taught there. Returning to England, he began work, sometime before 1616, to trace the circulation of the blood and in 1628 published his findings: that the heart pumps blood and that blood circulates to and from parts of the body through arteries and veins.

Many other scientists have helped decipher the functioning of the human body, that most intricate and vital of all mazes. Many of these scientists have focused on microscopic details of body machinery. It was left to the nineteenth-century surgeon, Sir Henry Gray, to produce a classical overall manual combining anatomy and surgical practice. Gray, long connected with St. George's Hospital, London, was famous in his day for his work on the retina, the endocrine glands, and the spleen. He is most famous in modern times and with class after class of medical students for his *Anatomy, Descriptive and Surgical* (1858), a lucidly written book with splendidly drawn illustrations.

The swift technological advances of modern times have profited all the sciences, but especially medicine. With new technology, the trained eye can see clearly into the human body. As is true of surgery and diagnostic medicine, the science of picturing human anatomy today is flourishing. Older techniques are combined with much newer approaches, to create a multiple view of several dimensions of the various body systems. This is the view afforded in *The Color Atlas of Human Anatomy*, which is not a medical text but is a summarized graphic and dramatic way of looking at the human body. Its appeal is to the intelligent layman.

Drawings, diagrams, and photographs in this atlas are illuminated by the newer knowledge, while some of them reflect older techniques, such as X-ray therapy. Diagnosticians have long used X-ray photography. Now they can add to their analytic aid computer-assisted tomography, known as CAT-scans. In these, an X-ray source is rotated through 180 degrees and the results conveyed to a computer. This has especially eased analysis of brain malfunction. Another new tool, the crystal scintillator, utilizing radioisotopes, produces scintigrams, looking rather like impressionistic wiggly-lined crewelwork and shown here mostly as bone scans.

Besides these radiologic tools, there are other new medical-analytical methods. Computer mapping of the body, by using two cameras clamped together to follow bodily contour lines, can show growth or response to therapy. Ultrasound, or sonar, can beam sound into body cavities and map the response. It can, for example, picture the fetus in the womb without injuring it.

Thermography, heat-sensitive photography, is particularly useful in locating tumors. With thermography, parts of the body appear as islands in surrounding seas of vivid color. In fact, the colors and patterns of the newer anatomical illustrations in *The Color Atlas* are often very beautiful.

The searching clinical eye can magnify and probe, also. The optical microscope and the powerful electron microscope extend sight into minute details. The glass fibers of endoscopy make it possible to see into a hollow human organ.

The book's generously illustrated description of the human body's anatomy and physiology begins with varieties of human tissue – muscle, bone, blood, spleen, lymphatic tissues. From there it proceeds to explain the locomotor systems (how bones and muscles work together); then, the circulation, the endocrine (glandular) system, the nerves, the special senses of sight, smell, taste, hearing, and touch, the respiratory system, the digestive system, and the urogenital system. Both color and black and white are used, but color work predominates. The text is brief, and an explanation nearly always applies to an illustration on the same double spread of pages.

To learn the language of anatomy, as illustrated here, broadens understanding of body processes and of diseases. How and why people shiver in winter, what are the causes and aspect of goiter, how does insulin affect metabolism, what are some of the new possibilities of correcting eye troubles, how are a child's tonsils and adenoids removed? Beyond demonstrating the complex wonder of our bodies, the atlas sheds light on these specific health problems and several more, while indicating the areas where science still finds human anatomy mysterious.

Above all, this pictorial presentation of anatomy can help make it clear to the lay reader how the muscles and nerves function, what is the course of food through the body, and other facets of the ordinary yet miraculous body mechanics and chemistry that govern everyday existence.

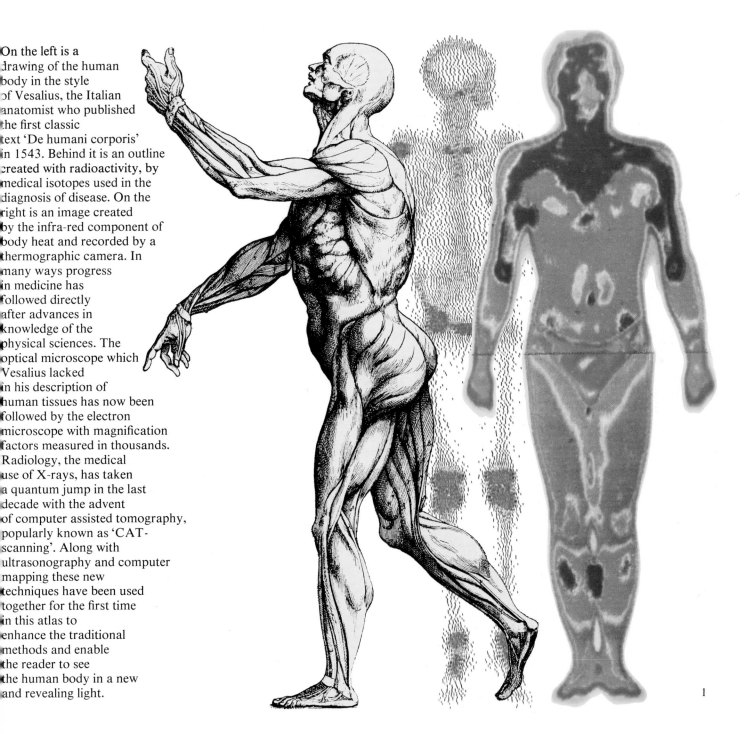

On the left is a
drawing of the human
body in the style
of Vesalius, the Italian
anatomist who published
the first classic
text 'De humani corporis'
in 1543. Behind it is an outline
created with radioactivity, by
medical isotopes used in the
diagnosis of disease. On the
right is an image created
by the infra-red component of
body heat and recorded by a
thermographic camera. In
many ways progress
in medicine has
followed directly
after advances in
knowledge of the
physical sciences. The
optical microscope which
Vesalius lacked
in his description of
human tissues has now been
followed by the electron
microscope with magnification
factors measured in thousands.
Radiology, the medical
use of X-rays, has taken
a quantum jump in the last
decade with the advent
of computer assisted tomography,
popularly known as 'CAT-
scanning'. Along with
ultrasonography and computer
mapping these new
techniques have been used
together for the first time
in this atlas to
enhance the traditional
methods and enable
the reader to see
the human body in a new
and revealing light.

1

the new methods of investigation

WITH LIGHT AND HEAT. We can run, jump, fight and, within certain limits, control the environment in which we live. It is the muscle mass of our bodies which grants these powers, some 501 different muscles distributed throughout the human form. With the naked eye a typical muscle can be seen to consist of two distinct parts – a white, tough extremity which is resilient, called the tendon, and a fleshy part or belly which is larger in the middle and is. the contracting part. The actual shapes of muscles vary enormously. They can be fusiform and simple; have two or three heads (bicipital and tricipital); be circular or flat and strap-like (sometimes with tendinous insertions as for the belly wall muscles) or they can be fan-shaped like the great pectoral muscles of the anterior chest wall. When shapes and relationships are carefully recorded, a traditional anatomical drawing such as the one below is the result. In order to further our knowledge we must penetrate deeper; the optical and electron microscopes provide detail about structure, while thermography and histochemistry (p. 15) yield information about function. By examining the underlying bones and joints (as well as following their nerve connections back towards the spinal cord and central nervous system) we can then begin to see the skeletal musculature as a complex but highly capable effector system responding to direct commands from the brain.

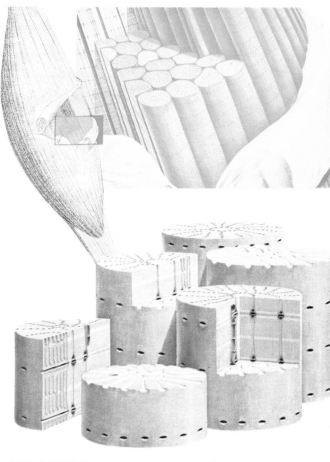

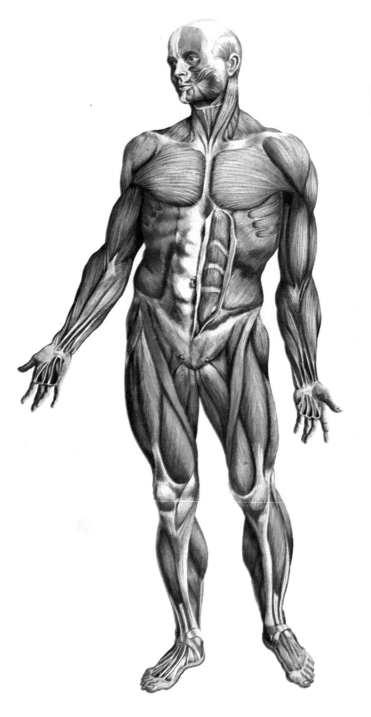

THE OPTICAL MICROSCOPE
With the optical microscope at low power we can see that the basic units of skeletal muscle are muscle fibers (top right) arranged in bundles of varying thickness within a fibrous outer covering. Each fiber has hundreds of nuclei and sometimes stretches from one end of the muscle to the other. With polarized light as the means of illumination and a higher magnification power (below right) the fibers show their own substructure of fine threads or myofibrils. In section these have a striated appearance, with alternating bands of dark and light color. Further examination of these striations using a high voltage electron microscope displays a regular network of filaments made up of two distinct proteins; actin and myosin (p. 15). The strands move towards each other during contraction, thus shortening the overall length of the muscle.

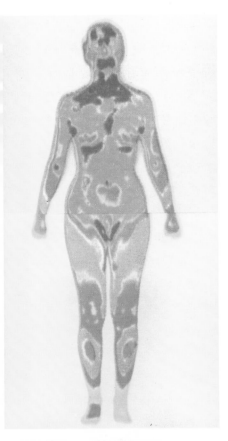
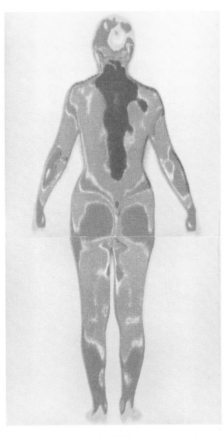

THERMOGRAPHY

This is a technique used to show up various body conditions in which the amount of heat emitted through the skin is altered. This heat is a by-product of the chemical reactions taking place in the tissues, but because the radiation wavelength is towards the infra-red end of the light spectrum, it is invisible to the unaided human eye. A relatively new instrument, the thermographic camera, can detect and record these emissions as a color which depends on the level of infra-red energy. To the left are anterior and posterior views of a normal individual in perfect health. The colors differ in various parts of the body, but the color changes are symmetrical. Notice the particular warmth of the scalp due to its excellent blood supply, and hence the great potential heat loss from an uncovered head in cold weather. Below left is the thermographic posterior view of a person with a severe spinal deformity. The scale at the lower edge of the picture is for color callibration. An X-ray picture (center) confirms the diagnosis before corrective treatment (right) is undertaken.

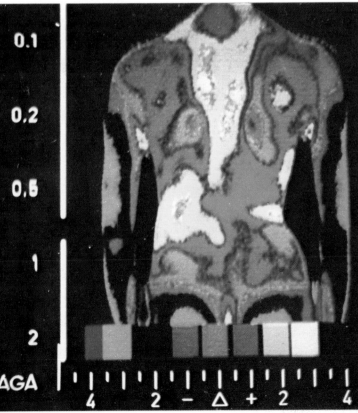
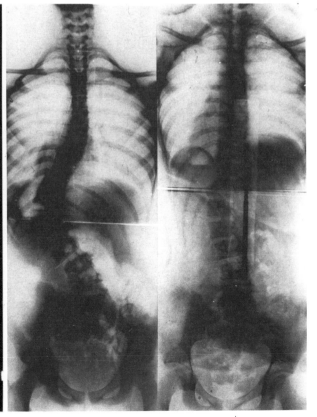

X-RAYS AND RADIOACTIVITY

The introduction into medical science of X-rays and (later) radio-isotopes as methods of investigation has made many hitherto difficult diagnoses much easier to achieve. Section of a long bone like the femur (below) shows its hollow cavity and delicate patterning, but this and the rest of the skeleton alongside become invisible when covered with muscles and skin. X-irradiation however, penetrates human tissues differently according to their density. Mineralized structures like bone cause almost complete absorption, in contrast to air-filled organs like the lungs through which the rays pass virtually unhindered. These densities can then be recorded on special photographic film. Certain radio-

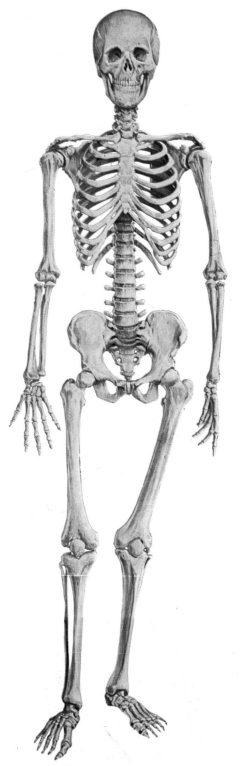

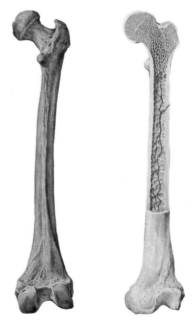

POLARIZED LIGHT microscopy shows the basic osteon units; concentric layers of thin bone crossed by a network of fine canals.

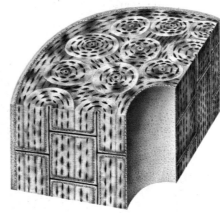

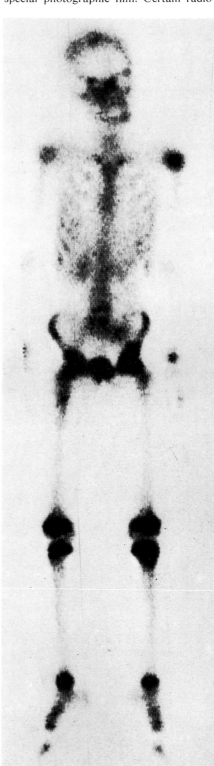

active isotopes are also selectively absorbed by bone when injected into the body and can therefore be used to outline normal and pathological bone conditions. The gamma ray emissions can be recorded by a special camera (facing page, right) or by using a scintillating crystal detector (this page) to produce a scintigram, or 'bone scan'. The center scintigram shows a normal child with very active growing zones located at the ends of the long bones. On the right there are multiple abnormal foci of radioactivity in the skull, ribs and spine. Their appearance is typical of secondary cancerous deposits, or metastases.

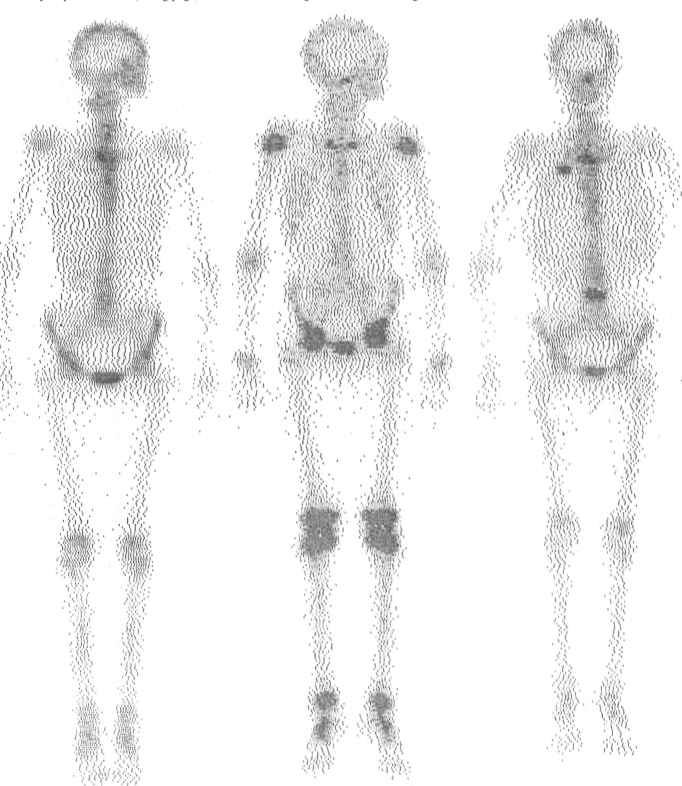

ULTRASOUND

A beam of very high frequency sound waves can be accurately directed into body cavities and a picture made of the reflections that result. This technique is also called 'sonar', and uses the same principles as those employed to map out the ocean depths or hunt submerged objects like submarines. It is the only method of investigating fetal well-being that carries no risk to the baby while it floats in the amniotic fluid. The drawing below shows how simple palpation of the pregnant uterus may be very misleading when the uterine wall is grossly distorted by fibroids. Below this are two ultrasound scan photographs of pregnancy together with outline diagrams to make them clearer. On the left the fetal parts are clearly seen beneath the placental shadow. The outline is normal, unlike that of the fetus on the right. At 22 weeks there is an excess of amniotic fluid and fetal abdominal distension caused by Rhesus disease. Sonar assistance is vital if this condition is to be treated by exchange blood transfusion.

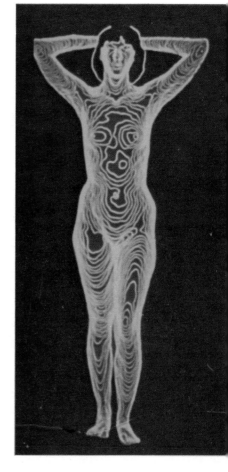

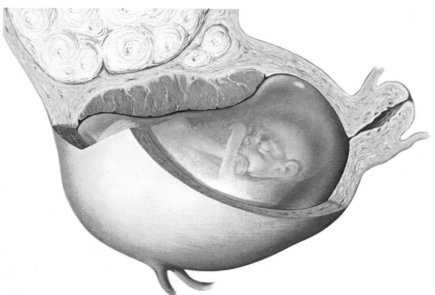

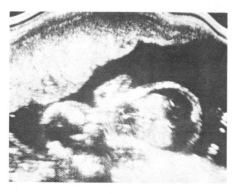

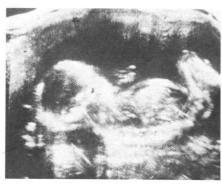

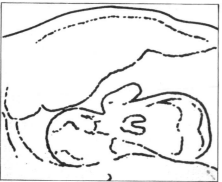

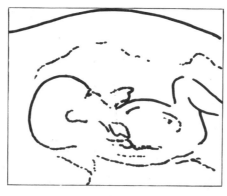

COMPUTER MAPPING OF THE BODY

Rather like the relief maps made from aerial photographs of the ground, this technique provides contour delineation of the structures in different parts of the human body. To make the map shown above, two cameras clamped together (but aligned at slightly different angles) moved down the long axis of the body in the same way that a survey aircraft flies along a given ground track. The contour lines were then electronically processed (above right) to give a clear picture and three-dimensional impression. The clinical use of body mapping is mainly restricted to orthopedic clinics. In studies of normal development it is possible with this method to measure the very small changes in shape and size associated with weekly growth, as well as quantifying the response to corrective therapy in clinical problems. On the right is a beautifully clear contour picture of a neonate to emphasize another aspect of this method – it is harmless, and can be repeated as often as necessary, without risk.

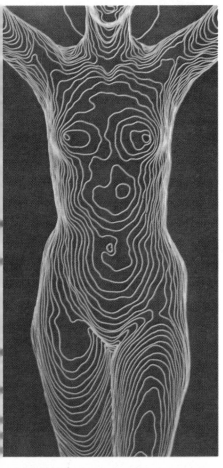

COMPUTER ASSISTED TOMOGRAPHY

This method is the very latest development in radiological investigation, especially that of the brain. It is non-invasive and accurate as well as quick. The CAT scanner consists of an X-ray source which rotates slowly through 180 degrees around the patient. Instead of a film, the X-rays strike a sensor plate which sends the impulses to a computer. This does the huge number of calculations necessary to drive a television display, and also stores the image in its memory. Left to right, top to bottom: a cranial section at eyeball level to show the crossing of the optic nerves; a thoracic 'slice' through the heart; the upper abdomen containing liver, pancreas and spleen; an enhanced view of lungs and pulmonary vessels; mid-abdomen with prominent kidney shadows and finally the pelvis, at hip joint level, with the air-filled rectum clearly visible in front of the sacrum.

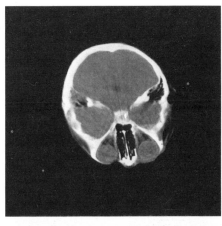

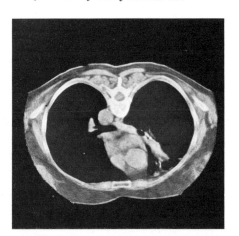

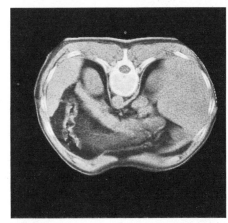

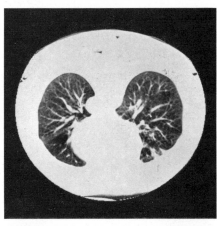

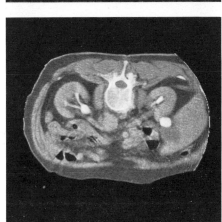

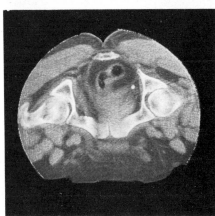

THE ELECTRON MICROSCOPE

Even with optical microscopic systems of the very highest quality there is a limit to their power of resolution, about three times greater than the size of the very smallest cellular components. But for the advent of electron microscopy (EM) many of the important details of cellular architecture discussed in the next section would have remained hidden. The earliest EM equipment demanded ultrathin preparations and plastic embedding media to hold them steady, so living cells could not be studied. A later development, the scanning electron microscope, has the electron beam focussed onto the surface of the specimen so that topography can be studied in very fine detail (right). The uppermost picture is in traditional style showing the relationship of the stomach to surrounding organs, including the liver which has been lifted away for clarity. Far right is a diagram that highlights the appearance of the gastric lining, while (center) we have a scanning EM photograph showing the individual mucosal cells and the openings of the deeper acid-secreting glands. Below, a diagram of the gall bladder, opened to display its honeycomb appearance. Lower center, a scanning EM photograph of the same structure, showing a pavement-like lining of simple columnar epithelium.

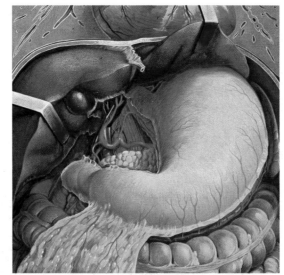

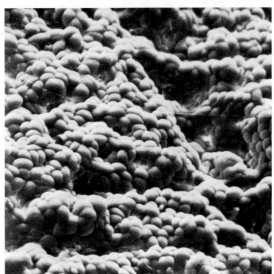

ENDOSCOPY is a technique of great clinical importance because it allows doctors to study the appearance and function of certain internal organs without resorting to major surgery. Bundles of glass fibers are carefully aligned into a flexible tube and connected to a viewing system. Light waves travelling down the tube are bounced back by total internal reflection, giving a very clear view in the best instruments. Biopsies can be taken for histological study. The esophagus, stomach and duodenum; the rectum and colon; the larynx, trachea and main bronchi; the urethra and bladder are now all areas that are easily accessible. If a small surgical incision has to be made in order to introduce the instrument, the procedure is termed laparoscopy; the picture of a cirrhotic liver (below) was obtained in this way.

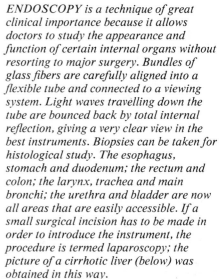

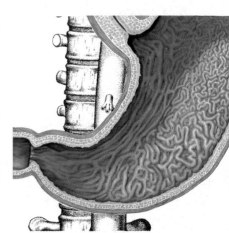

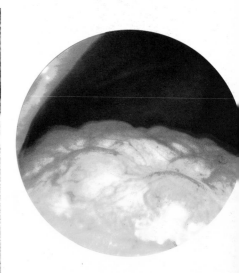

cells

Human beings, in common with all other living organisms, have a basic cellular substructure. The cell is the smallest living unit capable of growth, movement and reproduction. Cells that are specialized in function become bound together to form tissues, and in more complex creatures tissues become further aggregated as organs which display those specialized functions in a collective way. Whatever their origin, shape or size, cells are constantly being recreated from other cells by a complex process of division and replication called mitosis. A complete mitotic cycle is shown below: 1) breakup of the nuclear membrane; 2) the appearance of chromosomes (aggregations of genetic material) which 3) form 23 recognizable pairs, and then split. These line up 4) along the equator of the cell and 5) division of the cell protoplasm begins; progress is rapid 7) and 8) until separation is complete 9). There are now two daughter cells, each with a complete nucleus and 46 chromosomes. During the formation of reproductive cells such as spermatozoa and ova the process of cell division is different. Meiosis halves the chromosome number to 23, but at fertilization the total is restored to 46 and genetic information from both parents transferred to the child as a result. In warm blooded creatures the mitotic cycle takes between 15 and 20 minutes. Mitotic activity is especially heavy in cancerous cells. Cell survival times vary between a few minutes for certain intestinal cells to about 4 months for a red blood cell.

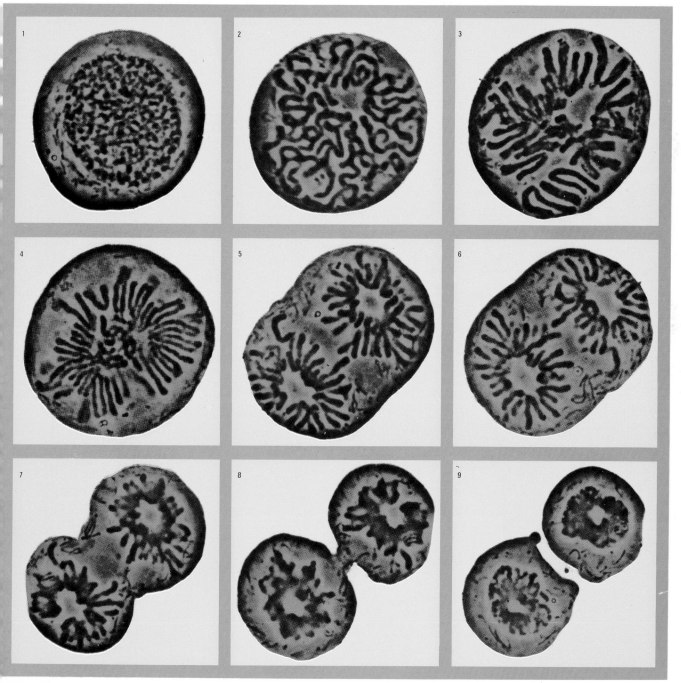

ribosomes

Golgi apparatus

nucleus

mitochondrion

nucleolus

endoplasmic
reticulum

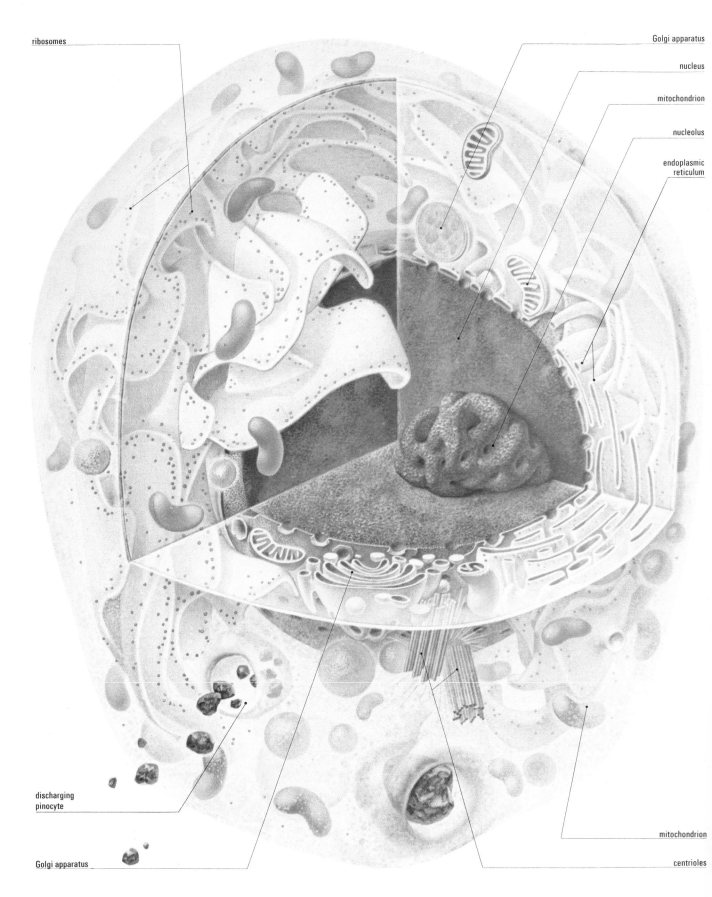

discharging
pinocyte

10 Golgi apparatus

mitochondrion

centrioles

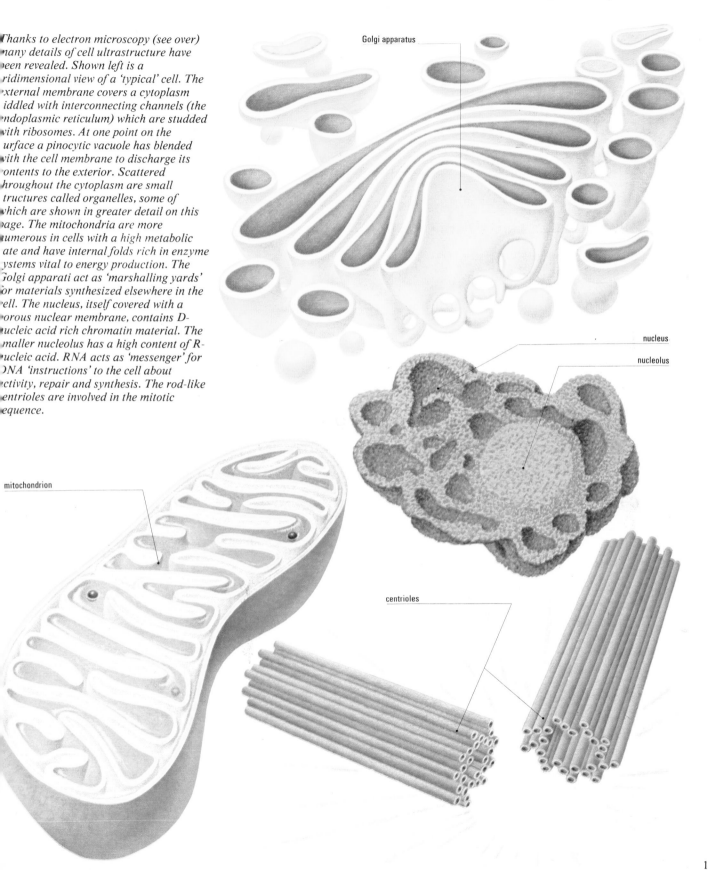

Thanks to electron microscopy (see over) many details of cell ultrastructure have been revealed. Shown left is a tridimensional view of a 'typical' cell. The external membrane covers a cytoplasm riddled with interconnecting channels (the endoplasmic reticulum) which are studded with ribosomes. At one point on the surface a pinocytic vacuole has blended with the cell membrane to discharge its contents to the exterior. Scattered throughout the cytoplasm are small structures called organelles, some of which are shown in greater detail on this page. The mitochondria are more numerous in cells with a high metabolic rate and have internal folds rich in enzyme systems vital to energy production. The Golgi apparati act as 'marshalling yards' for materials synthesized elsewhere in the cell. The nucleus, itself covered with a porous nuclear membrane, contains D-nucleic acid rich chromatin material. The smaller nucleolus has a high content of R-nucleic acid. RNA acts as 'messenger' for DNA 'instructions' to the cell about activity, repair and synthesis. The rod-like centrioles are involved in the mitotic sequence.

Golgi apparatus

nucleus

nucleolus

mitochondrion

centrioles

Throughout Nature there is an incredible variety of cell structure when related to function. This page shows several different examples. Upper left, a white cell precursor from salamander blood; to the right, a transected human cell displayed by electron microscopy. Compare the actual appearance with the diagrammatic representation on p. 11.

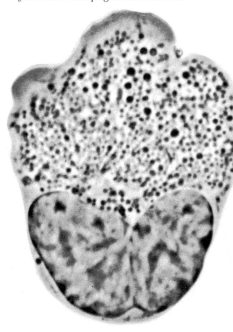

A plant cell layer showing nuclear mitotic activity; cell membranes have been stained pink in this optical microphotograph.

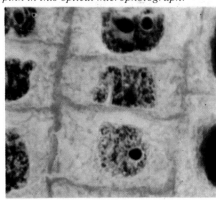

invagination of cell membrane

endoplasmic reticulum

nuclear membrane

nucleus

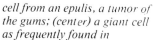

pinocytic vacuole

cell membrane

mitochondria

endoplasmic reticulum

Different pathological processes can cause considerable change in cell structure: (left) an enlarged polynuclear cell from an epulis, a tumor of the gums; (center) a giant cell as frequently found in sites of chronic inflammation and (right) varied mitotic figures in a tumor of nervous tissue.

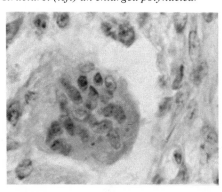

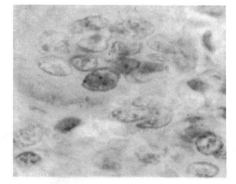

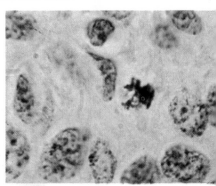

tissues

One classification of human tissues can be based conveniently on their origin. Three primitive cell types are identifiable in the embryo only a few weeks after implantation of the fertilized ovum. The ectoderm gives rise to the skin and adjoining mucous membranes, including the salivary glands, also the whole of the nervous system, the pituitary and adrenal medulla, the cornea and lens of the eye, and the neuro-epithelium of the other sense organs. From embryonic endoderm arise the lining of the alimentary tract together with the linings of all the 'glands' that open onto it (including liver and pancreas), the active cells of the thyroid, parathyroids and thymus, the lining cells of the lungs and air pas-

sages, and also the bladder and most of the urethra. All the connective and structural tissues like bone, muscle, blood and lymph derive from mesoderm, as well as the internal linings of the thoracic and abdominal cavities (pleura, pericardium and peritoneum). But this differentiation does not remain rigid. During growth of the embryo and the formation and development of its different organs, the separate cell layers can become intermingled at certain points. As a result, one structure or organ may display several separate functions. A common ectodermal origin allows us to understand how skin can become so intimately involved with sensory input to the central nervous

system. This perceptive function is further served by the inclusion of different specialist nerve cells to provide distinction between touch, pressure, warmth and pain. But skin has other functions too, including that of thermo-regulation. Sweat glands produce a fluid which cools the skin by evaporation; smooth muscle fibers of mesodermal origin are attached to hair follicles and can pull the hairs erect to minimise heat losses by forming a layer of still air. In addition, skeletal muscle fibers can contract under involuntary control to create the heat-generating phenomenon of shivering.

EPITHELIAL TISSUE *has the characteristic pattern of single or multiple cell layers resting on a basement membrane, functioning as* *selective barriers to deny access to some materials while admitting others (see next page). Human skin (below) represents a complex form of stratified* *epithelium, with a cornified and waterproof outer layer externally. This is ridged up, and perforated by sweat ducts and hair follicles.*

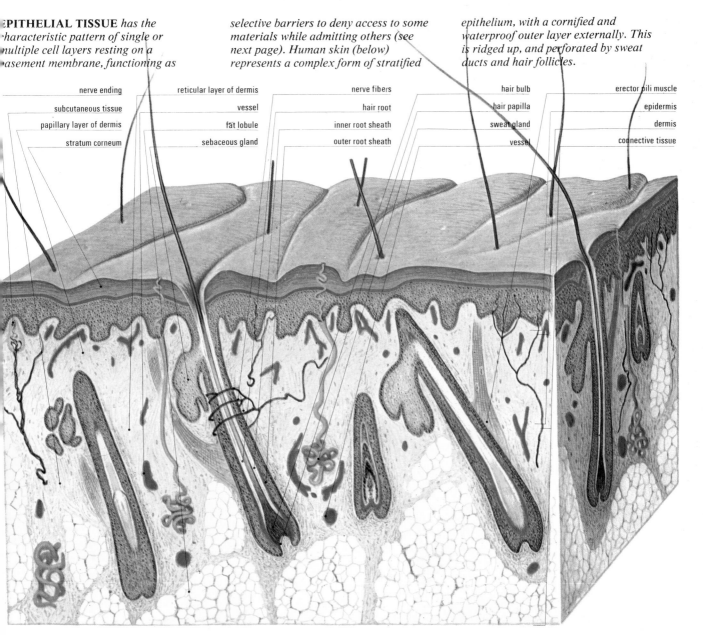

nerve ending
subcutaneous tissue
papillary layer of dermis
stratum corneum

reticular layer of dermis
vessel
fat lobule
sebaceous gland

nerve fibers
hair root
inner root sheath
outer root sheath

hair bulb
hair papilla
sweat gland
vessel

erector pili muscle
epidermis
dermis
connective tissue

An enlarged photomicrograph of human skin shows how the superficial stratum corneum degenerates and peels away, constantly being replaced by the darker staining epidermal layer beneath it. This type of epithelium is called stratified squamous; in simpler types the cells may be columnar or cuboidal in appearance. Exocrine secretory glands (like the sweat glands) show these cells lining tubular structures, often coiled, with ducts leading to the surface. Endocrine glands such as

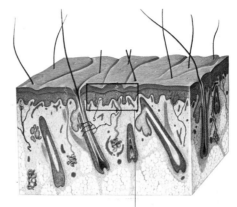

the adrenal medulla lose their ducts during development, so their secretions (hormones) have to travel via the blood-stream. A modified columnar epithelium lines the upper respiratory tract. The cells are elongated into beating cilia (diagram and microphotograph below) which have a constant protective function. Inhaled particles are trapped in the secretions of associated mucous glands and swept by ciliary movement up towards the pharynx to be ejected by coughing.

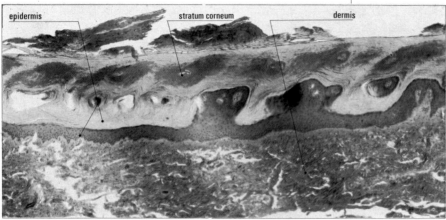

epidermis   stratum corneum   dermis

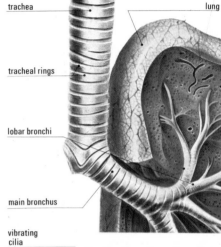

trachea   lung

tracheal rings

lobar bronchi

main bronchus

A variation in the temperature of the skin due to a pathological cause, shown by thermography (below).

Flat squamous cells shed by the moist vaginal skin (diagram above, microphotograph below).

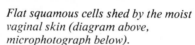

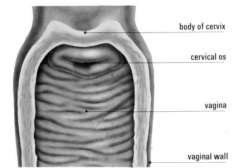

body of cervix

cervical os

vagina

vaginal wall

vibrating cilia

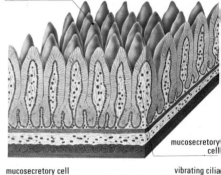

mucosecretory cell

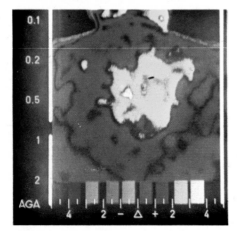

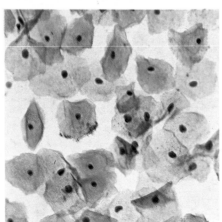

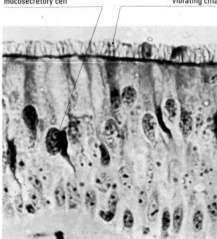

mucosecretory cell   vibrating cilia

Position (below) and histological appearance of a lobulated salivary type of glandular epithelium.

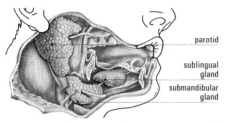

parotid

sublingual gland

submandibular gland

MUSCULAR TISSUE

As previously mentioned, this has contractile properties. Histologically, there are three kinds: striated (skeletal or voluntary), smooth (involuntary) and cardiac. Below is a highly stylised diagram to show how the contraction of myofibrils results from the formation of bridges between the specialist proteins myosin and actin, in the presence of calcium and phosphate ions and the energy molecules ADP and ATP.

inner circular

outer longitudinal

Smooth muscle fibers are found in most visceral organs, typically in inner and outer layers (diagram left). Unlike skeletal muscle these fibers are not striated, and remain independent of voluntary control (microphot. below).

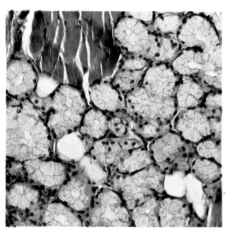

Diagram (below) and microphotograph of a secretory type of glandular epithelium found throughout the gut.

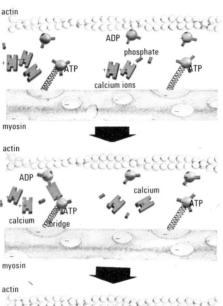

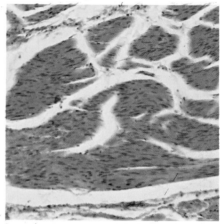

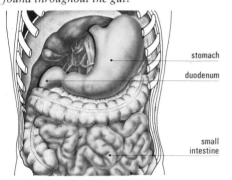

stomach

duodenum

small intestine

Skeletal muscle fibers (below) and an EM photograph (beneath) to show the striations and banding.

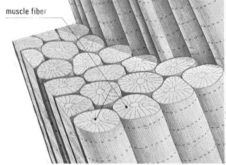

muscle fiber

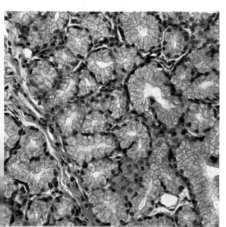

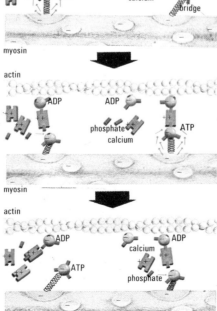

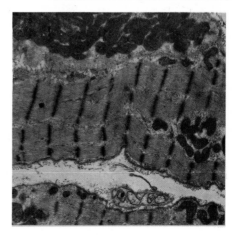

15

NERVE TISSUE
The human nervous system is incredibly complex and concerned with every aspect of our lives, in particular the body's reaction to changes in internal and external stimuli. The myriad pathways that make this possible are hinted at by the diagram (right). The neurons in cerebral tissue (diagram and microphotograph below) have numerous inter-dendritic connections and react to impulses caused by electro-chemical changes.

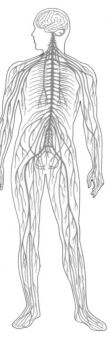

CONNECTIVE TISSUE
This is formed by two components, cells and an extra-cellular matrix. The matrix consists of viscous 'ground substance' and a varying number of collagen fibers. The cells may be fibroblasts; lymph or plasma cells; macrophages; fat or pigment cells. Needless to say, connective tissue is widely distributed throughout the body since it has structural and defensive functions. Some connective tissue becomes specialized in the structural role to form the skeletal tissues, cartilage and bone. Cartilage is tough and compact. In synovial joints it provides a slippery and wear resistant surface. Most skeletal bones have a cartilaginous precursor before the osteons appear, laying down concentric layers of bone called lamellae. These are rich in calcium phosphate crystals, and are placed around a vascular (Haversian) canal system (below).

BONE
Important not only from a structural point of view, or as a mineral reserve, long bones are hollow and the cavity contains marrow; this is a soft pulpy tissue from which red and white blood cells are produced. The two microphotographs are of myeloid cells labelled with an antibody and fluorescent dye.

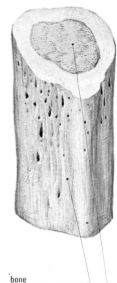

bone

marrow

dendrite

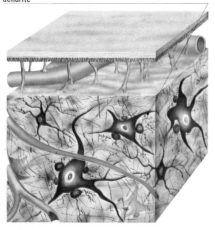

nerve fiber

cell body

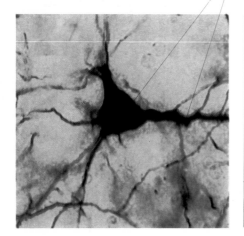

central canal

bone lamella

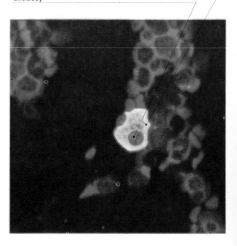

plasma cell

antibody

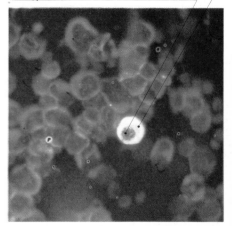

reticulum cell

antibody

bone lamella

BLOOD

Yet another type of connecting tissue specialized for transport and defense. There are 5 liters of blood in the adult circulation. The cellular components, whether red or white, are derived from a common 'stem' cell (see below) and are suspended in a protein rich fluid called plasma. Platelets are vital to blood clotting processes. The scanning electron microscope show red cells to be doughnut shaped envelopes (far right) containing hemoglobin, an iron rich specialist protein with a marked affinity for oxygen.

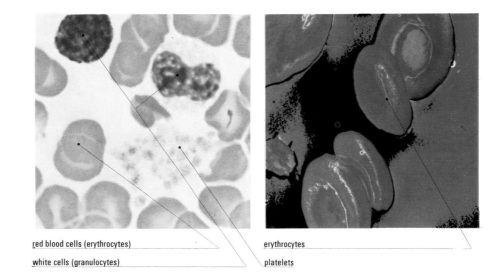

red blood cells (erythrocytes)

white cells (granulocytes)

erythrocytes

platelets

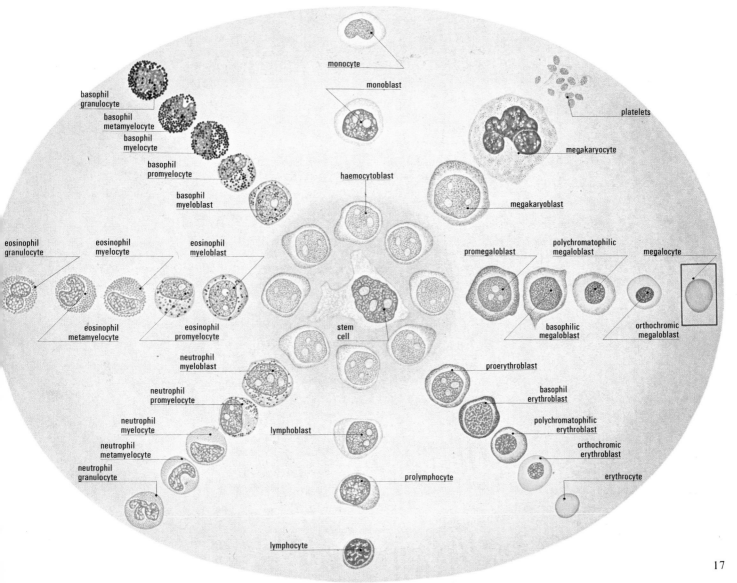

monocyte

monoblast

basophil granulocyte

basophil metamyelocyte

basophil myelocyte

basophil promyelocyte

basophil myeloblast

haemocytoblast

platelets

megakaryocyte

megakaryoblast

eosinophil granulocyte

eosinophil myelocyte

eosinophil myeloblast

eosinophil metamyelocyte

eosinophil promyelocyte

stem cell

promegaloblast

polychromatophilic megaloblast

megalocyte

basophilic megaloblast

orthochromic megaloblast

neutrophil myeloblast

neutrophil promyelocyte

neutrophil myelocyte

lymphoblast

proerythroblast

basophil erythroblast

polychromatophilic erythroblast

neutrophil metamyelocyte

neutrophil granulocyte

prolymphocyte

orthochromic erythroblast

erythrocyte

lymphocyte

17

THE SPLEEN

The spleen is located high up in the abdomen (illustr. right) under the left hemidiaphragm. It is involved in the creation, conservation and destruction of various blood elements, especially erythrocytes. Arterial blood circulates through the red splenic pulp which is rich in erythrocytes. Lymphatic tissue surrounding the smallest vessels forms the white pulp which is occasionally expanded into Malphigian corpuscles.

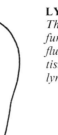

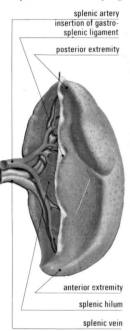

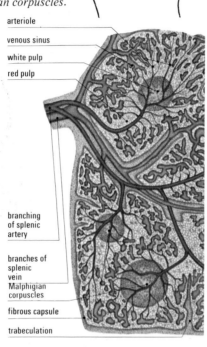

splenic artery
insertion of gastro-splenic ligament
posterior extremity

arteriole
venous sinus
white pulp
red pulp

branching of splenic artery

branches of splenic vein
Malphigian corpuscles

anterior extremity
splenic hilum
splenic vein

fibrous capsule
trabeculation

LYMPHATIC TISSUE

The lymphatic system has two functions – to drain lymph fluid formed in the peripheral tissues and to manufacture lymphocytes which are involved in body defensive processes. Bottom left, the distribution of lymphatic vessels; below, a lymph node in diagram and histological section.

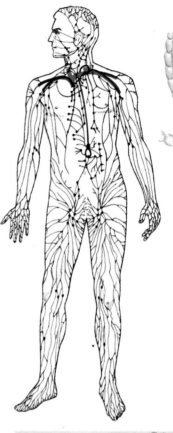

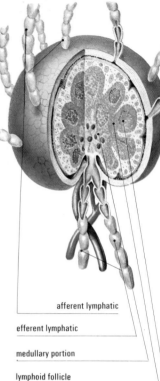

afferent lymphatic
efferent lymphatic
medullary portion
lymphoid follicle
germinal center

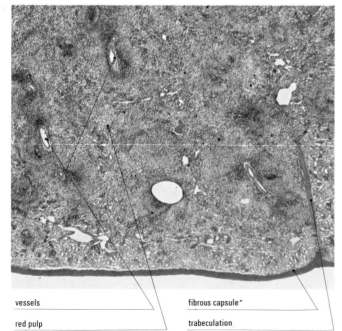

vessels
red pulp
fibrous capsule
trabeculation

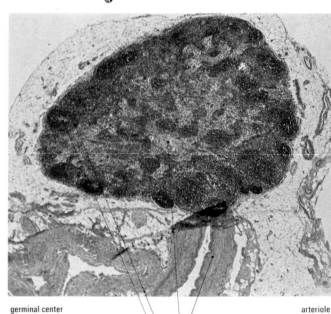

germinal center
lymphoid follicle

arteriole
medullary portion

the locomotor system

Some 208 skeletal bones act as the framework and 501 separate voluntary muscles provide the co-ordinated power that allow man to stand up and take charge of his environment. The basic features of bone and muscle tissue structure have already been mentioned; function can now be discussed. The bones generally act as a system of levers linked to each other by moveable connections, or joints. Joints vary widely in their structure and function. In the limbs the joints are highly mobile and lined with articular cartilage; the spinal column's movements are limited but sufficient, because of the way that the vertebral bodies are linked together. At the other extreme, the bones of the cranial vault are jointed, but completely immobile. The power and precision of the locomotor system is well demonstrated by the act of picking something up. Using locating information transmitted via optic pathways, the motor cortex (p. 52) co-ordinates shoulder, elbow and wrist movements until the extended fingers touch. Contact is signalled by touch receptors, and the joint positions then held while the fingers grasp the object and secure it. An increase in muscle power is then required to lift it, but with sufficient relaxation to allow the joints to move. This muscular co-ordination depends on the integrity of the cerebellum (p. 56) which is co-located with the base of the brain. It receives a constant stream of information from stretch and position receptors in muscles and joints along proprioceptive pathways, a rapid 'feedback' system allowing economy of orders. In addition, the cerebellum maintains muscular tone so that, even at rest, a muscle is ready for action. The final destination for its nerve impulses is the neuromuscular junction, a specialized structure on each muscle fibril. Acetylcholine released by the fine nerve endings crosses the gap to cause depolarization of the membrane. A spreading wave of chemical change causes the actin-myosin molecular links to shorten, and the muscle contracts. Muscular activity greatly increases the simple weight-bearing stresses on bony tissues. The tensile strength of bone is comparable to that of cast iron. A long bone like the femur (sectioned, right) shows cortical thickening to resist torsional strains in mid-shaft; at the hip the forces are mainly compressional, so the internal architecture is finely trabeculated along stress lines to reinforce and underpin the relatively thin cortex. The bones also constitute a mineral reserve for the body; disorders of calcium metabolism such as rickets and osteomalacia lead to characteristic deformities unless properly treated.

The complexity of the bony structures within the locomotor system is well demonstrated by the two figures below. On the left is the complete skeleton of an adult. The process of ossification has followed that of growth. On the right, the detailed structure of a long bone is displayed.

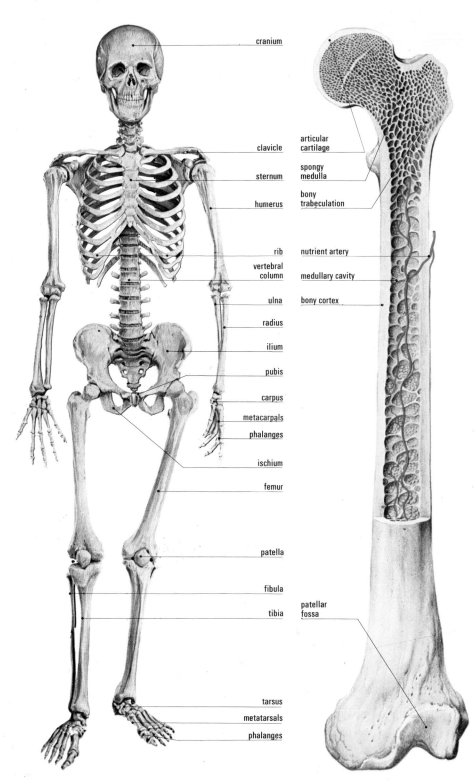

cranium

clavicle

sternum

humerus

rib

vertebral column

ulna

radius

ilium

pubis

carpus

metacarpals

phalanges

ischium

femur

patella

fibula

tibia

tarsus

metatarsals

phalanges

articular cartilage

spongy medulla

bony trabeculation

nutrient artery

medullary cavity

bony cortex

patellar fossa

19

bones

frontal bone

nasal bone

parietal bone

greater wing of sphenoid bone

lacrimal bone

temporal bone

zygomatic bone

inferior nasal concha

vomer

maxilla

mandible

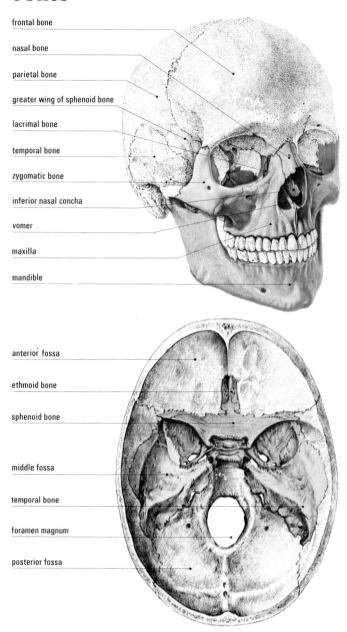

anterior fossa

ethmoid bone

sphenoid bone

middle fossa

temporal bone

foramen magnum

posterior fossa

On these pages, divested of their muscular coverings as well as their contents, are the skull, thorax and pelvis. For clarity, some of the bones making up the skull's complex framework (left, upper and middle) have been shown in different colors.

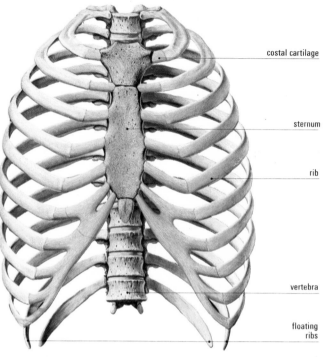

costal cartilage

sternum

rib

vertebra

floating ribs

Two diagrams of the pelvis: female (above) and male. *The broader dimensions of the female pelvic inlet* *are better adapted for passage of the fetal head during childbirth*

A CAT scan 'slice' through the posterior fossa. The nasal passages and maxillary sinuses are clearly visible as dark areas beneath the fainter outline of the foramen magnum; to each side of this are the air-filled cells of the mastoid bone.

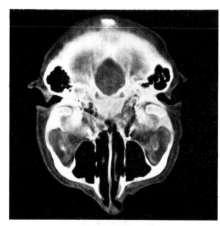

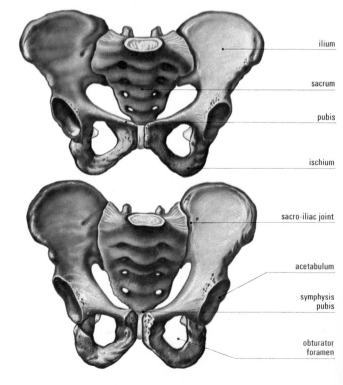

ilium

sacrum

pubis

ischium

sacro-iliac joint

acetabulum

symphysis pubis

obturator foramen

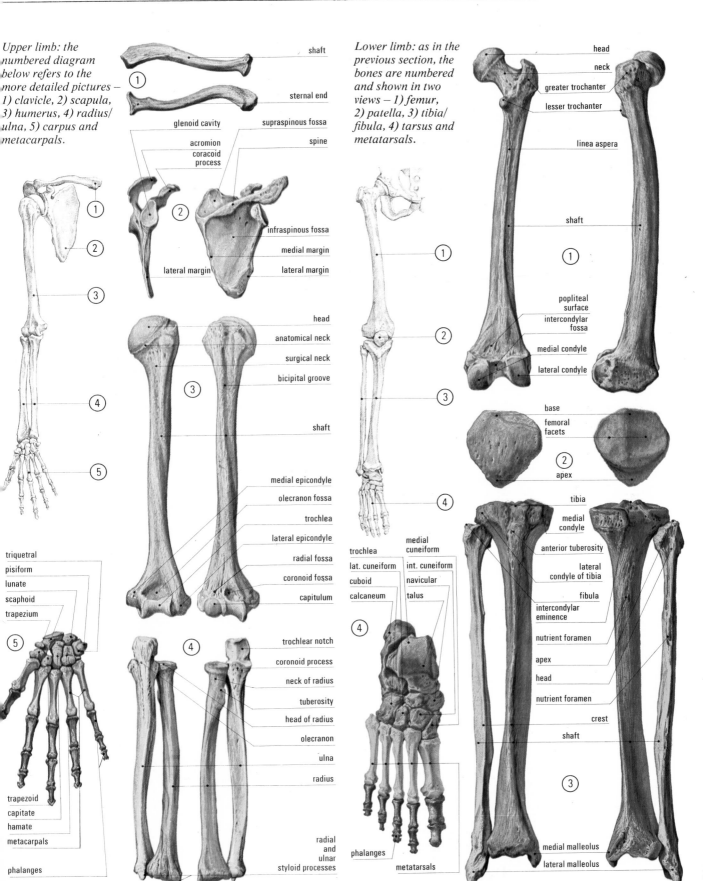

Upper limb: the numbered diagram below refers to the more detailed pictures – 1) clavicle, 2) scapula, 3) humerus, 4) radius/ulna, 5) carpus and metacarpals.

shaft

sternal end

glenoid cavity

supraspinous fossa

acromion

coracoid process

spine

infraspinous fossa

medial margin

lateral margin

lateral margin

head

anatomical neck

surgical neck

bicipital groove

shaft

medial epicondyle

olecranon fossa

trochlea

lateral epicondyle

radial fossa

coronoid fossa

capitulum

triquetral

pisiform

lunate

scaphoid

trapezium

trapezoid

capitate

hamate

metacarpals

phalanges

trochlear notch

coronoid process

neck of radius

tuberosity

head of radius

olecranon

ulna

radius

radial and ulnar styloid processes

Lower limb: as in the previous section, the bones are numbered and shown in two views – 1) femur, 2) patella, 3) tibia/fibula, 4) tarsus and metatarsals.

head

neck

greater trochanter

lesser trochanter

linea aspera

shaft

popliteal surface

intercondylar fossa

medial condyle

lateral condyle

base

femoral facets

apex

tibia

medial condyle

anterior tuberosity

lateral condyle of tibia

fibula

intercondylar eminence

nutrient foramen

apex

head

nutrient foramen

crest

shaft

medial malleolus

lateral malleolus

trochlea

lat. cuneiform

cuboid

calcaneum

medial cuneiform

int. cuneiform

navicular

talus

phalanges

metatarsals

21

In studying the diseases of bones and joints, whether localized problems or those resulting from more widespread disorders, there is one major problem with X-rays. At a certain total dosage, the amount depending on individual patient variation, there is a significant risk of developing radiation induced diseases such as leukemia. Although radioisotopes also emit radiation in clinical use, the amounts involved are very small thanks to their short half-life and the high sensitivity of detectors such as the crystal scintillator and the gamma camera. The former produces

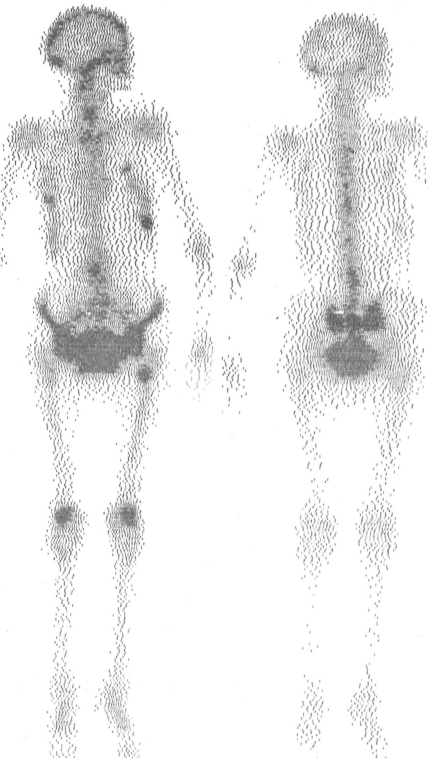

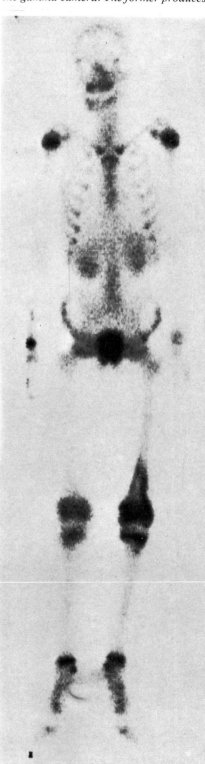

a scintigram (below left, two examples) and the latter a photo-negative (below, remaining four pictures) with density proportional to the level of radioactivity. The scintigrams are anterior and posterior views of a normal child. The middle pair of gamma photographs are also of a healthy child. Note how radioisotope excreted in the urine has, in the posterior view, produced a strong image of the kidneys. On the right is a child with osteomyelitis. There are multiple foci of hyperactivity in the upper thorax and neck.

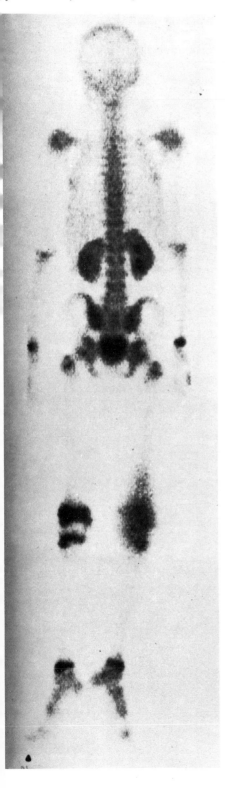
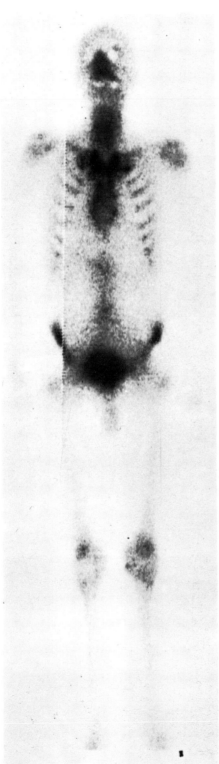
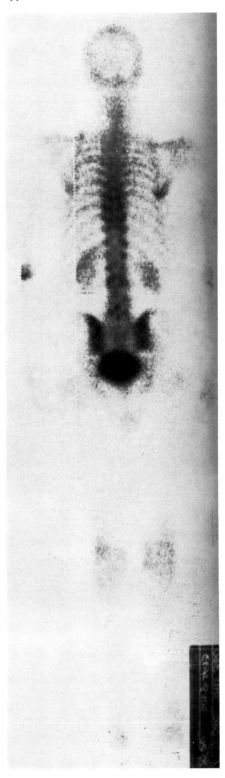

In the accurate diagnosis of serious bone disorders such as malignant tumors, X-rays reign supreme. Thermography has a valuable function in its rapidity of screening; since the blood flow through a fast growing tumor is greater than through normal tissue, the amount of infra-red energy radiated is also increased. This is well shown in the accompanying examples. If surgery is contemplated in order to remove a malignancy, then it is also important for the surgeon to know the exact blood supply. In the technique of angiography, a radio-opaque dye is injected into the main artery while serial X-rays are taken. The vessels in the two angiograms on this page are shown as white lines of diminishing caliber.

Below, an angiogram and thermographic image of a bone tumor of the upper arm. Both techniques have localized the site of the lesion accurately, but the fine detail of the X-ray further suggests an osteosarcoma of the humerus. However, the other pictures provide examples of the thermographic images being more clearly recognizable as abnormal than the radiographic ones: (upper middle) an angiogram of the popliteal artery and tibial shaft tumor, and (upper right) an expanding tumor of the first metatorsal bone. Both sets of thermographs render the underlying circulatory disturbances vividly clear, especially when color modulated.

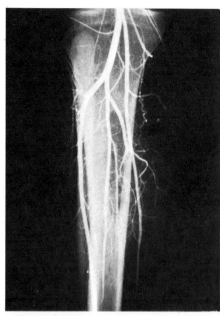
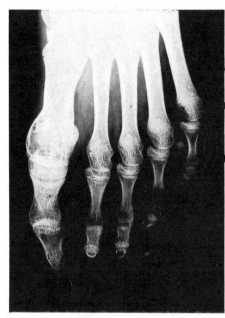

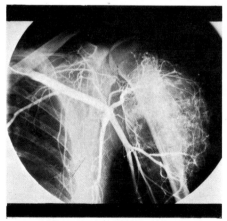

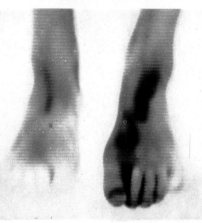

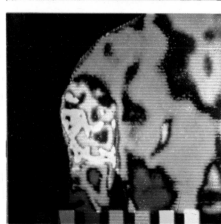
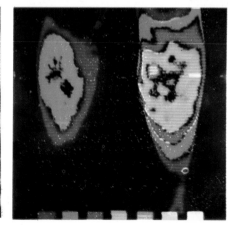
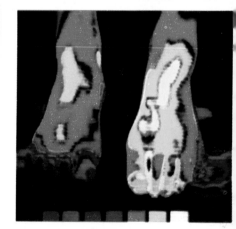

muscles

The muscle mass is not just concerned with locomotion. It assists in the circulation of blood and protects and confines the visceral organs. It also provides the main shaping component of the human form. A detailed knowledge of myology is of vital importance to doctors, especially surgeons because, having established the surface anatomy and exact location of an organ, they must plan the best access route to give minimum risk to the patient. On this page are the principal muscles of the anterior and posterior aspects of the body.

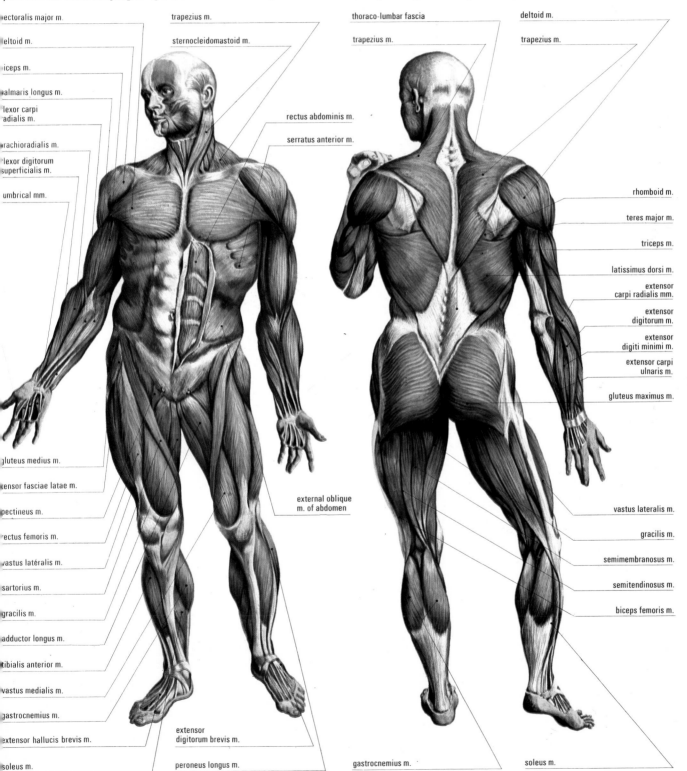

pectoralis major m.

deltoid m.

biceps m.

palmaris longus m.

flexor carpi radialis m.

brachioradialis m.

flexor digitorum superficialis m.

lumbrical mm.

gluteus medius m.

tensor fasciae latae m.

pectineus m.

rectus femoris m.

vastus lateralis m.

sartorius m.

gracilis m.

adductor longus m.

tibialis anterior m.

vastus medialis m.

gastrocnemius m.

extensor hallucis brevis m.

soleus m.

trapezius m.

sternocleidomastoid m.

rectus abdominis m.

serratus anterior m.

external oblique m. of abdomen

extensor digitorum brevis m.

peroneus longus m.

thoraco-lumbar fascia

trapezius m.

gastrocnemius m.

deltoid m.

trapezius m.

rhomboid m.

teres major m.

triceps m.

latissimus dorsi m.

extensor carpi radialis mm.

extensor digitorum m.

extensor digiti minimi m.

extensor carpi ulnaris m.

gluteus maximus m.

vastus lateralis m.

gracilis m.

semimembranosus m.

semitendinosus m.

biceps femoris m.

soleus m.

Electron microscopy of skeletal muscle (below) shows the cross section of a myofibril; the thick dots are myosin threads with smaller actin filaments arranged around them, linked by cross-bridges. To the left of the photograph are two sectioned mitochondria. A special cell membrane provides electrical continuity (diagram right) between the neuromuscular junction and the rest of the fibril.

Skeletal muscle masses tend to be grouped or layered according to their tasks. This feature is readily apparent in the following four pages, where careful dissection at different planes of depth reveals an astonishing variety of form. Below left are the facial muscles which have the additional higher function of expressing emotion. Below, the superficial musculature of the chest and trunk, in anterior and posterior views.

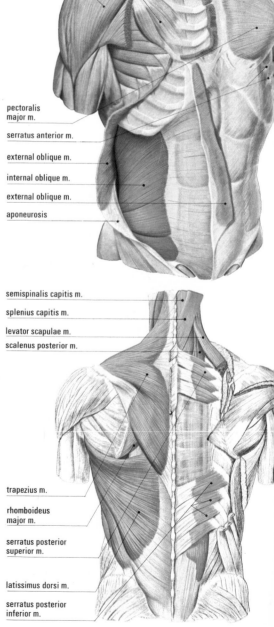

pectoralis minor m.

deltoid m.

pectoralis major m.

serratus anterior m.

external oblique m.

internal oblique m.

external oblique m.

aponeurosis

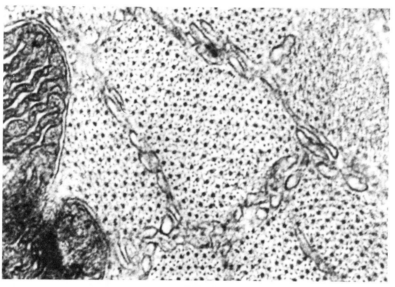

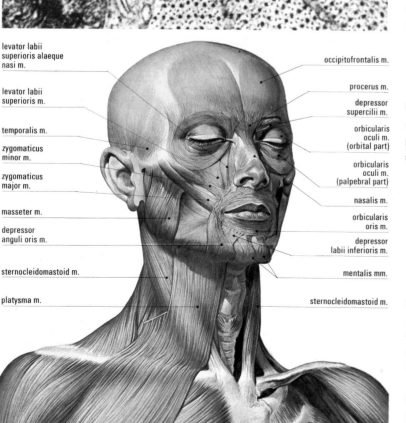

levator labii superioris alaeque nasi m.

levator labii superioris m.

temporalis m.

zygomaticus minor m.

zygomaticus major m.

masseter m.

depressor anguli oris m.

sternocleidomastoid m.

platysma m.

occipitofrontalis m.

procerus m.

depressor supercilii m.

orbicularis oculi m. (orbital part)

orbicularis oculi m. (palpebral part)

nasalis m.

orbicularis oris m.

depressor labii inferioris m.

mentalis mm.

sternocleidomastoid m.

semispinalis capitis m.

splenius capitis m.

levator scapulae m.

scalenus posterior m.

trapezius m.

rhomboideus major m.

serratus posterior superior m.

latissimus dorsi m.

serratus posterior inferior m.

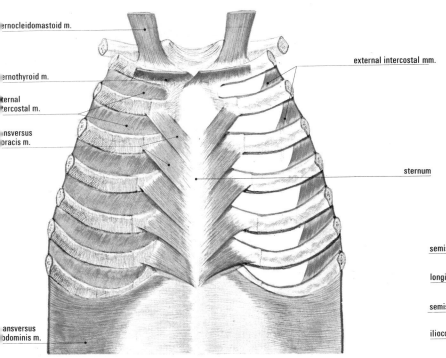

ernocleidomastoid m.

ernothyroid m.

ternal
tercostal m.

nsversus
oracis m.

ansversus
bdominis m.

external intercostal mm.

sternum

To the left, the deep muscles of the chest wall which are involved in movements of the ribs. Below (left and right) are the deepest layers of the abdomen and trunk. The multiple insertions of dorsal muscles into ribs and vertebrae allow for precision in control as well as considerable flexibility in twisting movements of the trunk. The fibers of the intercostal muscles both run obliquely, but at right angles to each other; their actions in increasing thoracic volume during respiration will be discussed in more detail on p. 78.

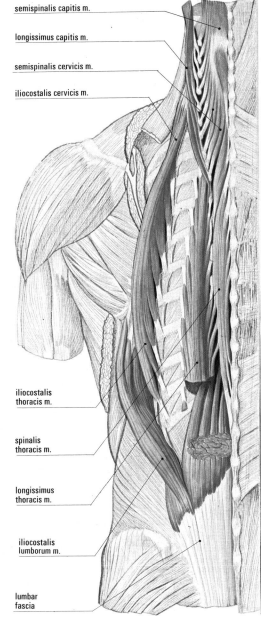

semispinalis capitis m.

longissimus capitis m.

semispinalis cervicis m.

iliocostalis cervicis m.

iliocostalis
thoracis m.

spinalis
thoracis m.

longissimus
thoracis m.

iliocostalis
lumborum m.

lumbar
fascia

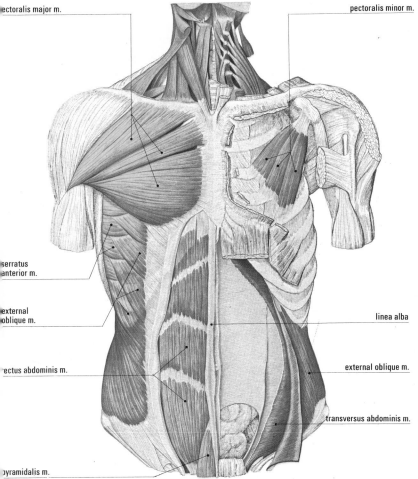

ectoralis major m.

pectoralis minor m.

serratus
anterior m.

external
oblique m.

ectus abdominis m.

yramidalis m.

linea alba

external oblique m.

transversus abdominis m.

27

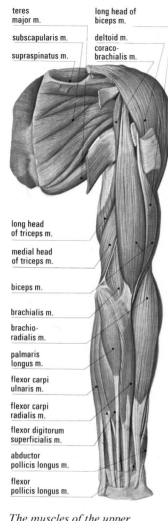

teres major m.
long head of biceps m.
subscapularis m.
deltoid m.
coraco-brachialis m.
supraspinatus m.
long head of triceps m.
medial head of triceps m.
biceps m.
brachialis m.
brachio-radialis m.
palmaris longus m.
flexor carpi ulnaris m.
flexor carpi radialis m.
flexor digitorum superficialis m.
abductor pollicis longus m.
flexor pollicis longus m.

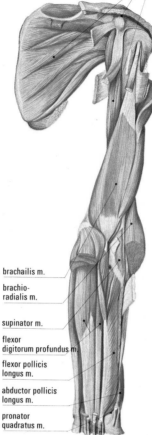

coracobrachialis m.
deltoid m.
subscapularis m.
brachailis m.
brachio-radialis m.
supinator m.
flexor digitorum profundus m.
flexor pollicis longus m.
abductor pollicis longus m.
pronator quadratus m.

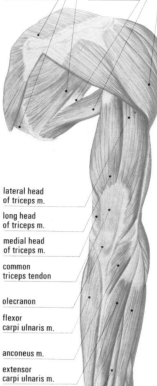

infraspinatus m.
rhomboideus major m.
trapezius m.
deltoid m.
teres major m.
teres minor m.
lateral head of triceps m.
long head of triceps m.
medial head of triceps m.
common triceps tendon
olecranon
flexor carpi ulnaris m.
anconeus m.
extensor carpi ulnaris m.
extensor digitorum m.
extensor digiti minimi m.

infraspinatus m.
teres minor m.
supraspinatus m.
teres minor m.
long head of triceps m.
scapula
deltoid m.
long head of triceps m.
lateral head of triceps m.
medial head of triceps m.
biceps m.
brachio-radialis m.
supinator m.
abductor pollicis longus m.
extensor pollicis longus m.
extensor indicis m.
ulna
extensor pollicis brevis m.

The muscles of the upper limb can be divided into four groups; shoulder, arm, forearm and hand. Above, the left arm and

scapula are shown detached from the thorax, in superficial and deep layers. Opposite, a similar dissection of the

right arm, this time from a posterior aspect. The shoulder girdle forms a strong yet mobile base for the arm; because this can fold and

also ends in a powerful precision tool (the hand, below) the upper limb display a very great range and versatility of movement.

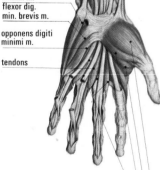

abductor digiti minimi m.
flexor dig. min. brevis m.
opponens digiti minimi m.
tendons
lumbrical mm.
flexor pollicis brevis m.
adductor pollicis m.
abductor pollicis brevis m.

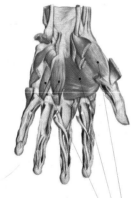

interosseous mm.
adductor pollicis m.
opponens pollicis m.

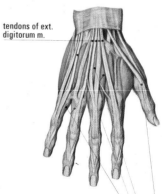

tendons of ext. digitorum m.
phalanges
tendons of ext. digitorum m.
dorsal interosseous mm.
tendon of ext. pollicis longus m.

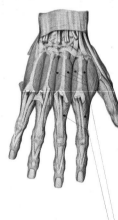

phalanges
dorsal interosseous mm.

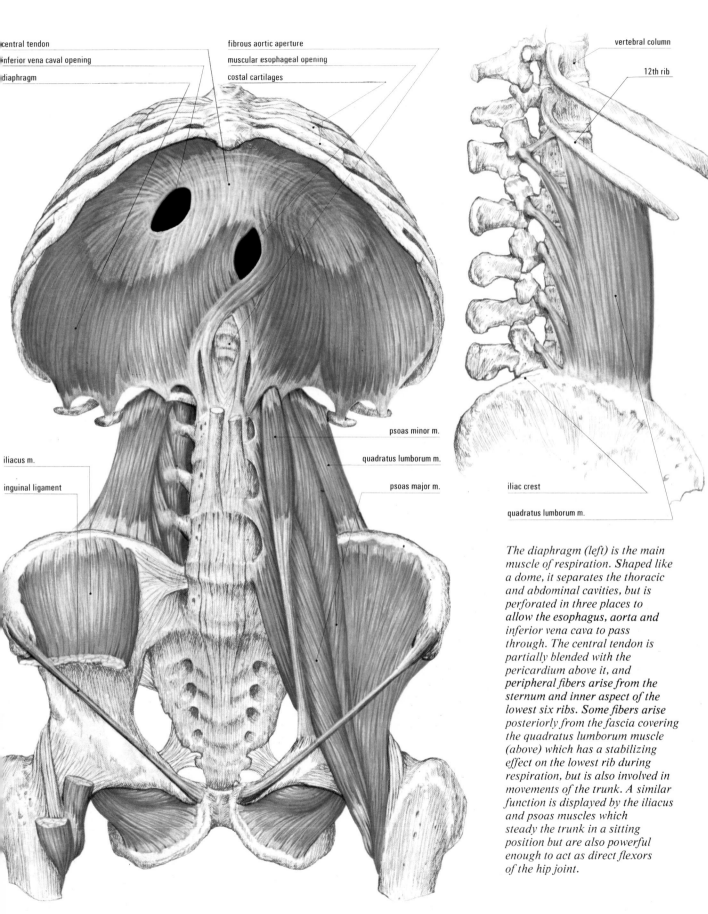

central tendon

inferior vena caval opening

diaphragm

fibrous aortic aperture

muscular esophageal opening

costal cartilages

vertebral column

12th rib

psoas minor m.

quadratus lumborum m.

iliacus m.

inguinal ligament

psoas major m.

iliac crest

quadratus lumborum m.

The diaphragm (left) is the main muscle of respiration. Shaped like a dome, it separates the thoracic and abdominal cavities, but is perforated in three places to allow the esophagus, aorta and inferior vena cava to pass through. The central tendon is partially blended with the pericardium above it, and peripheral fibers arise from the sternum and inner aspect of the lowest six ribs. Some fibers arise posteriorly from the fascia covering the quadratus lumborum muscle (above) which has a stabilizing effect on the lowest rib during respiration, but is also involved in movements of the trunk. A similar function is displayed by the iliacus and psoas muscles which steady the trunk in a sitting position but are also powerful enough to act as direct flexors of the hip joint.

29

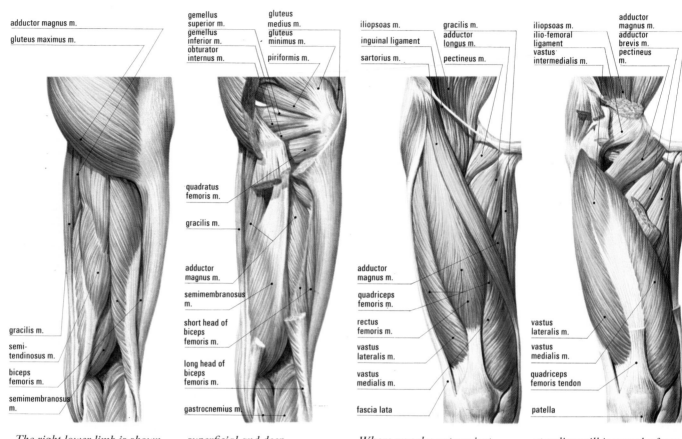

adductor magnus m.

gluteus maximus m.

gracilis m.

semi-
tendinosus m.

biceps
femoris m.

semimembranosus
m.

gemellus
superior m.
gemellus
inferior m.
obturator
internus m.

gluteus
medius m.
gluteus
minimus m.

piriformis m.

quadratus
femoris m.

gracilis m.

adductor
magnus m.

semimembranosus
m.

short head of
biceps
femoris m.

long head of
biceps
femoris m.

gastrocnemius m.

iliopsoas m.

inguinal ligament

sartorius m.

gracilis m.
adductor
longus m.

pectineus m.

adductor
magnus m.

quadriceps
femoris m.

rectus
femoris m.

vastus
lateralis m.

vastus
medialis m.

fascia lata

iliopsoas m.
ilio-femoral
ligament
vastus
intermedialis m.

adductor
magnus m.
adductor
brevis m.
pectineus
m.

vastus
lateralis m.

vastus
medialis m.

quadriceps
femoris tendon

patella

*The right lower limb is shown
above and below in the same
manner as the upper limb
(p. 28); posterior and then
anterior views are presented in*

*superficial and deep
dissections. The femur can move
in any axis thanks to powerful
musculature acting on the
ball-and-socket hip joint (p. 32).*

*Where muscles act against
gravity (eg. the glutei in
abduction of the thigh) their
bulk tends to be greater. The
body's center of gravity when*

*standing still is over the front
the ankle joint; the posterior
(calf) muscles and their action
of plantar flexion become vital
the maintenance of erect postu*

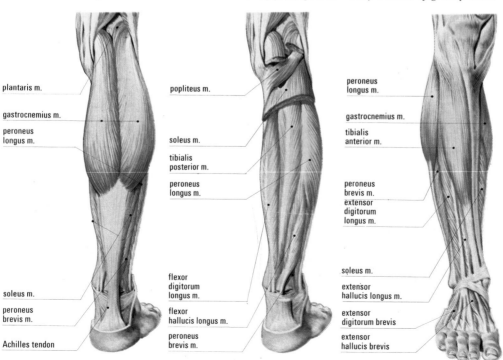

plantaris m.

gastrocnemius m.

peroneus
longus m.

soleus m.

peroneus
brevis m.

Achilles tendon

popliteus m.

soleus m.

tibialis
posterior m.

peroneus
longus m.

flexor
digitorum
longus m.

flexor
hallucis longus m.

peroneus
brevis m.

peroneus
longus m.

gastrocnemius m.

tibialis
anterior m.

peroneus
brevis m.
extensor
digitorum
longus m.

soleus m.

extensor
hallucis longus m.

extensor
digitorum brevis

extensor
hallucis brevis

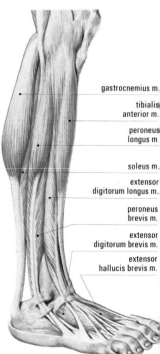

gastrocnemius m.

tibialis
anterior m.

peroneus
longus m

soleus m.

extensor
digitorum longus m.

peroneus
brevis m.

extensor
digitorum brevis m.

extensor
hallucis brevis m.

30

Joints

The junctions between various components of the skeletal framework have a variety of names – arthroses, articulations or joints. Traditionally they are classified according to structure (which has marked relation to function): fibrous, or fixed; cartilaginous or semi-mobile; synovial, or freely movable. In synovial joints, although the articulating bones are linked by a fibrous capsule and frequently reinforced and strengthened by associated ligaments, the actual joint surfaces are lubricated by a sticky fluid with a low co-efficient of friction. Occasionally the loading of the joint and its lubrication may be assisted by the inclusion of a disc or meniscus (the knee), or strengthened by an intra-articular ligament (the hip).

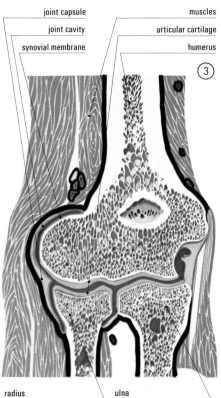

superior
gleno-humeral ligt.
coraco-
humeral ligt.
transverse
humeral ligt.

inferior
gleno-humeral ligt.
middle
gleno-humeral ligt.

①

joint capsule
joint cavity
synovial membrane
muscles
articular cartilage
humerus

③

On the skeletal outline (left) the joints have been circled, numbered, and then enlarged on this and the following page: 1) anterior view of shoulder, 2) section through thoracic vertebral and costovertebral joints, 3) the elbow in sectioned and anterolateral views.

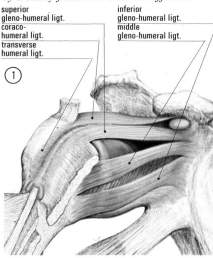

supraspinous ligt.
interspinous ligt.
vertebral
spinous process
costo-transverse
ligaments

②

vertebral arch
rib
intra-
articular ligament
vertebral body
nucleus pulposus

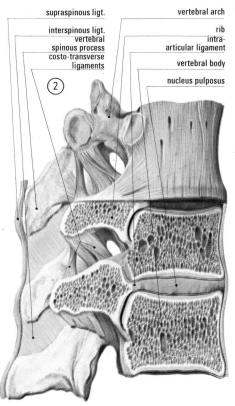

radius   ulna

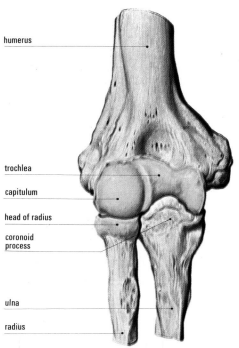

humerus

trochlea
capitulum
head of radius
coronoid
process

ulna
radius

31

The carpometacarpal joints of the hand (no. 4 in skeletal diagram) are shown sectioned (below). The joint at the base of the thumb, between the first metacarpal and trapezium, has a separate joint capsule and synovial lining. The thumb is highly mobile because of the design of this joint and its many associated muscles.

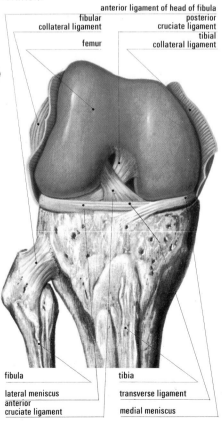

metacarpals

carpus

④

The robust multi-axial hip joint (no. 5 in diagram) is shown in section (below) and disarticulated (below right). The depth of the acetabular fossa is considerably

hyaline cartilage

joint cavity

joint capsule

muscles

muscles

synovial membrane

femoral head

pelvis

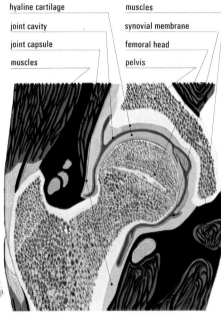

increased by a fibro-cartilaginous ring. The joint capsule is thick and tough: giving extra stability, an intra-articular ligament is sheathed by synovial membrane.

⑤

hyaline cartilage

acetabular fossa

ligamentum teres

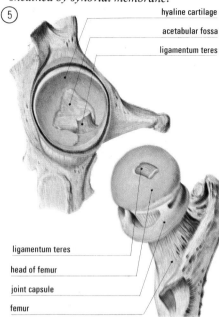

ligamentum teres

head of femur

joint capsule

femur

The knee (no. 6) is shown (below) in transverse section, and (below right) flexed, with the patella removed for clarity. It is the largest joint

synovial membrane

anterior cruciate ligament

transverse ligament

femur

tibia

pretibial bursa

patella

prepatellar bursa

in the body. The movements made by the tibia during extension are complex, and involve an element of rotation.

anterior ligament of head of fibula

fibular
collateral ligament

posterior
cruciate ligament

femur

tibial
collateral ligament

⑥

fibula

lateral meniscus

anterior
cruciate ligament

tibia

transverse ligament

medial meniscus

The tarsometatarsal joints of the foot are synovial; the articulating surfaces are almost flat. Movements between the bones are restricted and of a gliding type, but the first metatarsal's functions are slightly more versatile. The tarsal joints are vital in maintaining proper contact with the ground even when walking or running. This strong but flexible base is also contributed to by the curved shape of the medial and lateral bony arches.

⑦

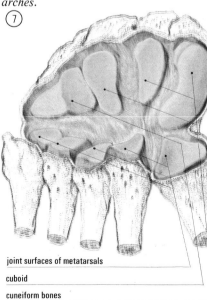

joint surfaces of metatarsals

cuboid

cuneiform bones

the circulation

The continued existence of the many cells which make up human tissues is dependent on an adequate circulation; this provides the oxygen essential for metabolic processes and also removes the carbon dioxide formed as a waste product. The cardiovascular system is hydraulic since the transport medium is blood. A mechanical double pump (the heart) pulses the fluid at high pressure through a series of tubes (arteries and arterioles) which become smaller until virtually cell size (capillaries); a collecting system of lower pressure (venules and veins) then returns de-oxygenated blood for a separate circulation via the right side of the heart and through the lungs. With oxygen content restored and carbon dioxide levels reduced by loss in expired air, the blood begins the whole circuit once again. The distribution vessels of the arterial tree show considerable variation in microscopic structure. Close to the heart, elastic fibers predominate to absorb the peak pressures of the systolic phase and smooth them out; closer to the tissues the flow of blood is more even (although still pulsatile) and here smooth muscle fibers predominate. These are under nervous control (p. 62) and so offer a peripheral resistance with a direct and variable effect on blood pressure; this feature can also provide a selective distribution system to direct blood flow towards tissue masses with the greatest physiological needs (eg skeletal muscle during hard exercise). The capillaries act as exchange vessels; Through their thin walls pass oxygen, carbon dioxide, water, ions and various metabolic products. Where inflammation occurs the defensive (white) phagocytic cells can also cross the barrier. The residual pressure at this level also helps in the formation of lymph fluid within tissue spaces; this is eventually returned, after passing through the lymphatic system (p. 40) to the right side of the heart. The venous system acts as a large volume reservoir of low pressure. The amount of blood returning to the heart (venous return) must be carefully controlled; the output of both left and right sides (despite the huge pressure differences between systemic and pulmonary circulations) must remain the same, and there is a direct relationship between venous return and cardiac output. The blood which returns from the stomach and intestines (and also the pancreas and spleen) is returned directly to the liver instead of the right side of the heart. The hepatic cells efficiently extract the rich products of digestion for their own vital purposes here, rather than waiting for their arrival in the arterial supply. This secondary circulation constitutes a portal system. There is another portal circulation associated with the pituitary gland (p. 43).

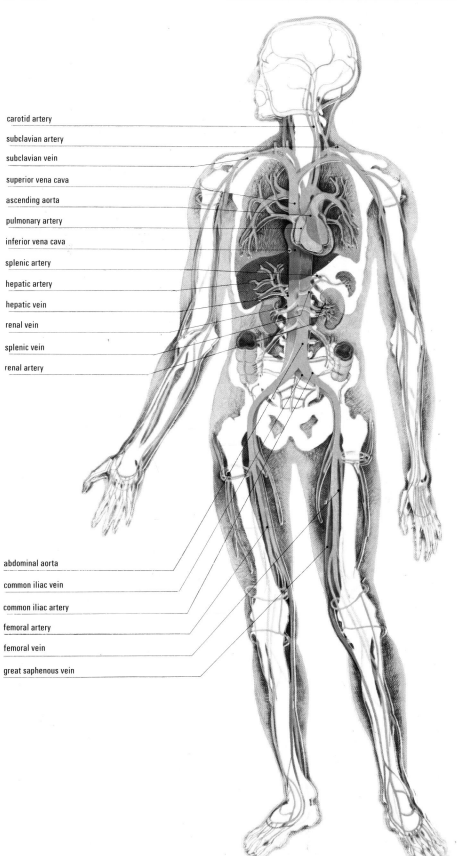

carotid artery

subclavian artery

subclavian vein

superior vena cava

ascending aorta

pulmonary artery

inferior vena cava

splenic artery

hepatic artery

hepatic vein

renal vein

splenic vein

renal artery

abdominal aorta

common iliac vein

common iliac artery

femoral artery

femoral vein

great saphenous vein

33

the heart

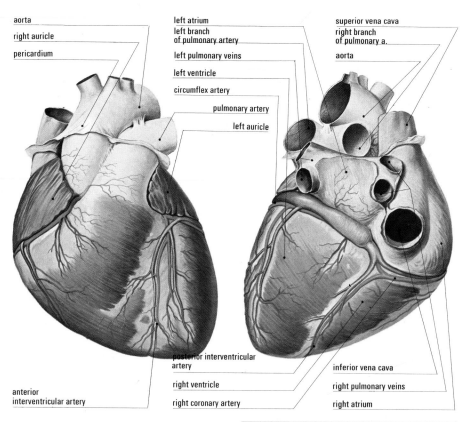

aorta
right auricle
pericardium

left atrium
left branch of pulmonary artery
left pulmonary veins
left ventricle
circumflex artery
pulmonary artery
left auricle

superior vena cava
right branch of pulmonary a.
aorta

anterior interventricular artery

posterior interventricular artery
right ventricle
right coronary artery

inferior vena cava
right pulmonary veins
right atrium

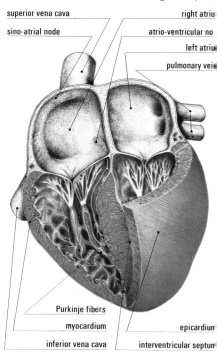

The exterior features of the heart are revealed (left and middle) in anterior and posterior views; the impulse conducting mechanism is shown in two diagrams (belo

superior vena cava
sino-atrial node

right atriu
atrio-ventricular no
left atriu
pulmonary vei

Purkinje fibers
myocardium
inferior vena cava

epicardium
interventricular septum

The heart is basically a hollow muscular organ weighing approximately 300 gm. It is divided into four chambers (below) and covered by two layers of pericardium. The right and left sides are separated by septa; the tricuspid and mitral valves respectively prevent backflow into the upper chambers, while pulmonary and aortic valves guard against reflux from the outflow tracts. A CAT scan through the thorax (right) shows the valvular structure in fine detail. Although striated, cardiac muscle has unique properties. Some fibers have been modified to form an electrical conducting system to co-ordinate the expulsive ventricular effort of systole. Even if this is defective, the heart will still beat slowly due to its inherent rhythmicity. A complete cardiac cycle (below) shows the atria filled with

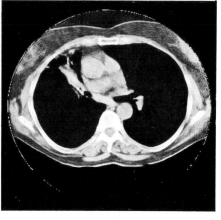

systemic (blue – deoxygenated) and pulmonary (red – oxygenated) venous blood; these contract and fill the ventricles through the atrioventricular (AV) valves.

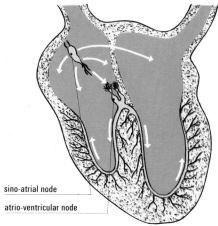

sino-atrial node
atrio-ventricular node

Diastole gives way to systole as the ventricles contract, close the AV valves, and pump the blood out via the pulmonary arteries and ascending aorta.

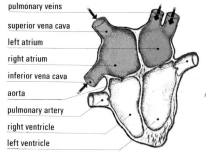

pulmonary veins
superior vena cava
left atrium
right atrium
inferior vena cava
aorta
pulmonary artery
right ventricle
left ventricle

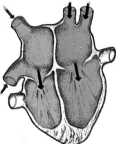
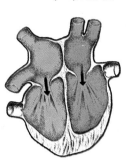
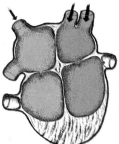
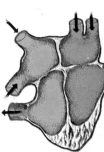

The mechanical sequence of a cardiac cycle can be followed externally by recording the associated electrical activity as an electrocardiogram. The trace (right) begins at an electrically neutral (isoelectric) level interrupted by atrial contraction (P wave). The ventricular contraction produces a much bigger peak (QRS complex) followed by repolarization of the myocardium (T wave) ready for the next cycle. The EKG has great clinical importance; disorders of rhythm and damage to the conducting system (or the myocardium itself) produce easily recognizable EKG changes. In certain conditions the heart can be driven externally using a battery operated electrode or 'pacemaker'.

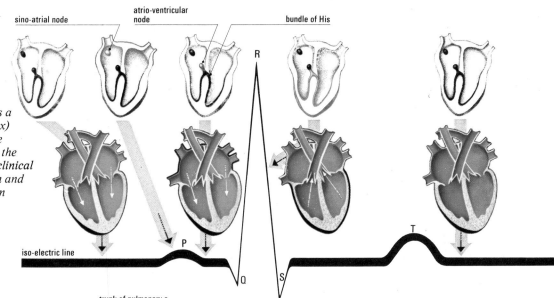

sino-atrial node · atrio-ventricular node · bundle of His

R

P · Q · S · T

iso-electric line

superior vena cava
right pulmonary vein
aorta
trunk of pulmonary a.
left pulmonary vein

right atrium
right ventricle
inferior vena cava
left atrium
left ventricle

In the fetal circulation the lungs are inactive; a flap valve allows mixing of the blood in the left ventricular chamber, but this valve closes soon after the first breath is taken. Some cardiac malformations cause cyanosis (blue babies) due to improper oxygenation of arterial blood. Fallot's tetralogy (above and right) is an example; the stenosed pulmonary artery, ventricular septal defect, malpositioned aorta and right ventricular hypertrophy are all characteristic, but usually correctable by surgery.

The blood supply of the heart itself comes from two coronary arteries; these can become blocked to produce myocardial ischemia. If severe, cardiac standstill will result; occasionally recanalization through the thrombosed area (below) may occur.

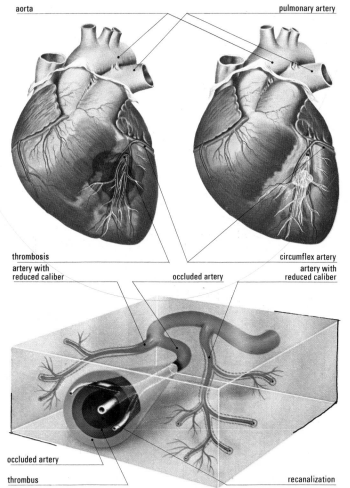

aorta
pulmonary artery

thrombosis
artery with reduced caliber
occluded artery
circumflex artery
artery with reduced caliber

occluded artery
thrombus
recanalization

35

vessels

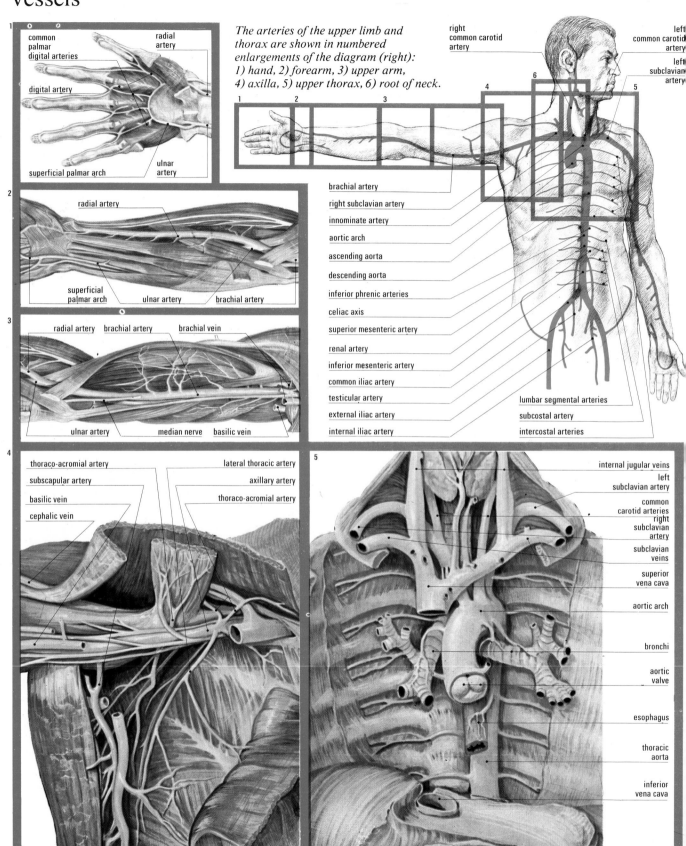

1

common palmar digital arteries

radial artery

digital artery

superficial palmar arch

ulnar artery

2

radial artery

superficial palmar arch   ulnar artery   brachial artery

3

radial artery   brachial artery   brachial vein

ulnar artery   median nerve   basilic vein

4

thoraco-acromial artery

subscapular artery

basilic vein

cephalic vein

lateral thoracic artery

axillary artery

thoraco-acromial artery

The arteries of the upper limb and thorax are shown in numbered enlargements of the diagram (right):
1) hand, 2) forearm, 3) upper arm,
4) axilla, 5) upper thorax, 6) root of neck.

right common carotid artery

left common carotid artery

left subclavian artery

1   2   3   4   6   5

brachial artery

right subclavian artery

innominate artery

aortic arch

ascending aorta

descending aorta

inferior phrenic arteries

celiac axis

superior mesenteric artery

renal artery

inferior mesenteric artery

common iliac artery

testicular artery

external iliac artery

internal iliac artery

lumbar segmental arteries

subcostal artery

intercostal arteries

5

internal jugular veins

left subclavian artery

common carotid arteries
right subclavian artery

subclavian veins

superior vena cava

aortic arch

bronchi

aortic valve

esophagus

thoracic aorta

inferior vena cava

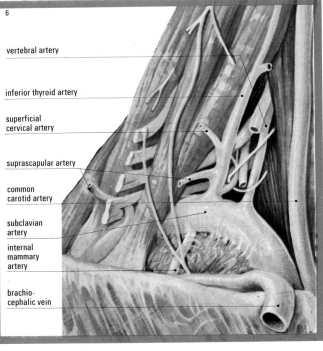

6

vertebral artery

inferior thyroid artery

superficial
cervical artery

suprascapular artery

common
carotid artery

subclavian
artery

internal
mammary
artery

brachio-
cephalic vein

The abdominal aorta divides at
the level of the fourth lumbar
vertebra into two common iliac
arteries (below): these in turn
divide into internal and external
branches. The internal iliac
artery has anterior and posterior
divisions to supply the pelvic
contents, genitalia and buttock
muscles. The external iliac artery
continues under the inguinal
ligament to form the femoral artery.

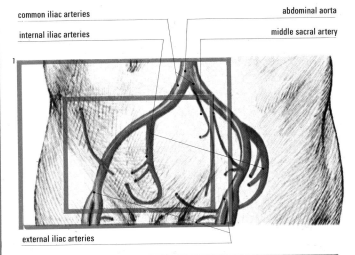

common iliac arteries

internal iliac arteries

abdominal aorta

middle sacral artery

1

external iliac arteries

The common carotid artery
bifurcates at the upper border
of the thyroid cartilage to form
internal and external branches.
The internal carotid continues

upwards to the base of the
brain where it forms an
anastomotic arterial circle
(of Willis) with the vertebral
vessels.

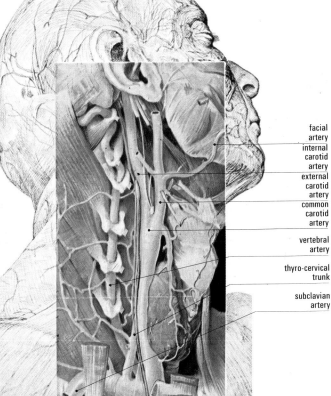

facial
artery

internal
carotid
artery

external
carotid
artery

common
carotid
artery

vertebral
artery

thyro-cervical
trunk

subclavian
artery

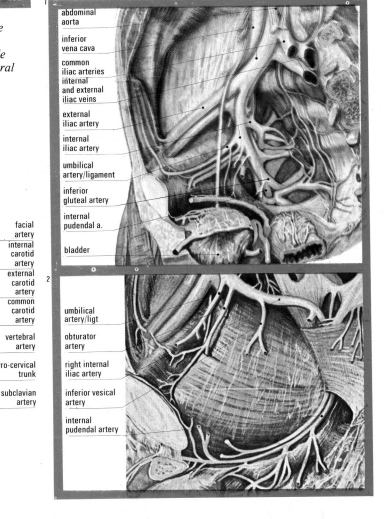

1

abdominal
aorta

inferior
vena cava

common
iliac arteries

internal
and external
iliac veins

external
iliac artery

internal
iliac artery

umbilical
artery/ligament

inferior
gluteal artery

internal
pudendal a.

bladder

2

umbilical
artery/ligt

obturator
artery

right internal
iliac artery

inferior vesical
artery

internal
pudendal artery

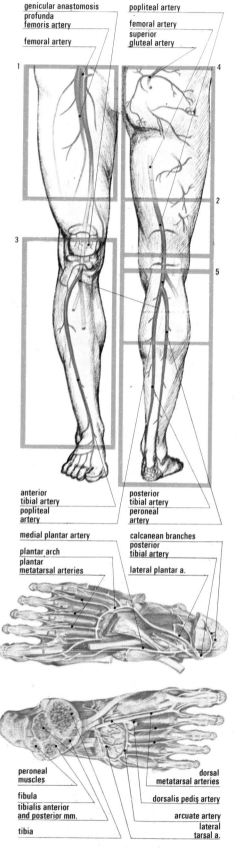

genicular anastomosis
profunda femoris artery
femoral artery

popliteal artery
femoral artery
superior gluteal artery

anterior tibial artery
popliteal artery

posterior tibial artery
peroneal artery

medial plantar artery
plantar arch
plantar metatarsal arteries

calcanean branches
posterior tibial artery
lateral plantar a.

peroneal muscles
fibula
tibialis anterior and posterior mm.
tibia

dorsal metatarsal arteries
dorsalis pedis artery
arcuate artery
lateral tarsal a.

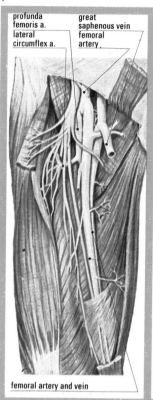

1
profunda femoris a.
lateral circumflex a.
great saphenous vein
femoral artery

femoral artery and vein

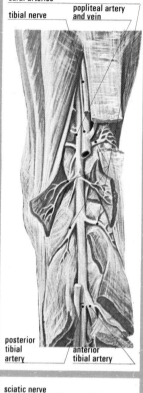

2
genicular and sural arteries
tibial nerve
popliteal artery and vein

posterior tibial artery
anterior tibial artery

3
deep peroneal nerve
common peroneal n.

anterior tibial artery

The arterial supply of the lower limb is shown (left) in anterior and posterior views, with enlargements of detail. The main vessel is the femoral continuation of the external iliac. In the thigh it runs in a canal beneath the sartorius muscle. There is a rich arterial anastomosis around the knee joint formed by three pairs of genicular vessels; below the knee, at the level of popliteus it divides into anterior and posterior tibial branches. The anterior tibial passes forwards to lie on the interosseous membrane between tibia and fibula; after entering the foot it ends by forming the dorsalis pedis artery (left). The posterior tibial gives off a peroneal branch before medial and lateral plantar terminals join to form a deep arterial arch.

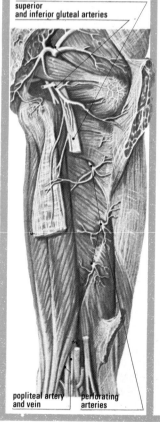

4
sciatic nerve
superior and inferior gluteal arteries

popliteal artery and vein
perforating arteries

5
popliteal vein
popliteal artery
posterior tibial artery
peroneal artery

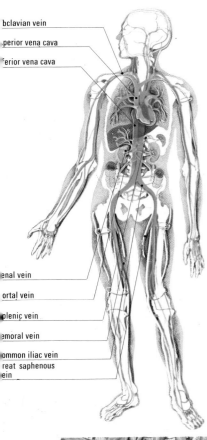

- bclavian vein
- perior vena cava
- ferior vena cava
- enal vein
- ortal vein
- plenic vein
- emoral vein
- ommon iliac vein
- reat saphenous vein

The systemic veins return blood from the peripheral tissues to the heart. Their superficial anatomy is very variable, but the deep veins generally accompany arteries.

The diagrams show the veins of the head and neck, upper and lower limbs, root of neck, pelvis and (lower left) the inner aspect of the posterior thoracic wall.

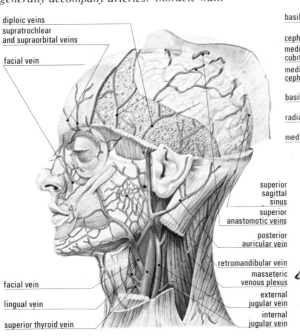

- diploic veins
- supratrochlear and supraorbital veins
- facial vein
- facial vein
- lingual vein
- superior thyroid vein
- superior sagittal sinus
- superior anastomotic veins
- posterior auricular vein
- retromandibular vein
- masseteric venous plexus
- external jugular vein
- internal jugular vein

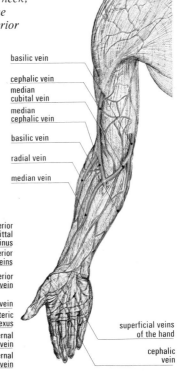

- basilic vein
- cephalic vein
- median cubital vein
- median cephalic vein
- basilic vein
- radial vein
- median vein
- superficial veins of the hand
- cephalic vein

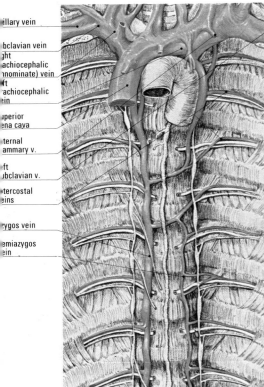

- illary vein
- bclavian vein
- ght achiocephalic nnominate) vein
- ft achiocephalic ein
- uperior ena cava
- nternal ammary v.
- ft ubclavian v.
- tercostal eins
- zygos vein
- emiazygos ein

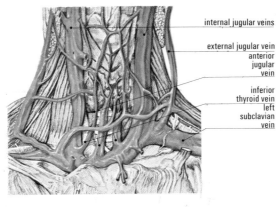

- internal jugular veins
- external jugular vein
- anterior jugular vein
- inferior thyroid vein
- left subclavian vein

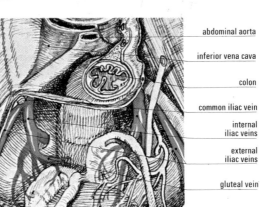

- abdominal aorta
- inferior vena cava
- colon
- common iliac vein
- internal iliac veins
- external iliac veins
- gluteal vein

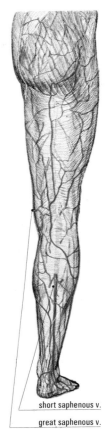

- short saphenous v.
- great saphenous v.

39

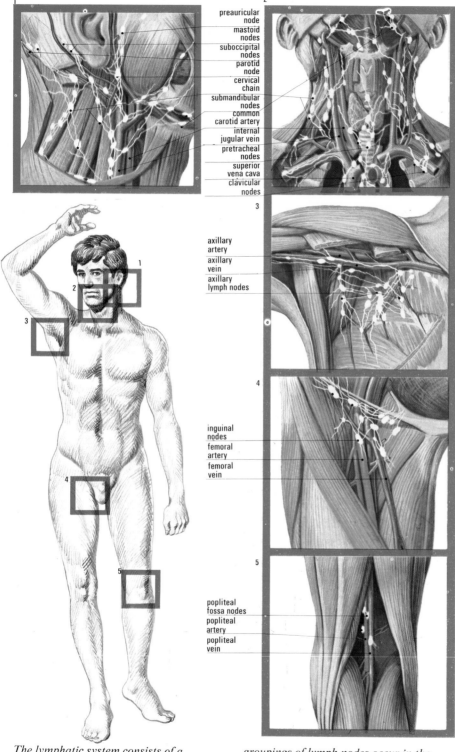

preauricular
node
mastoid
nodes
suboccipital
nodes
parotid
node
cervical
chain
submandibular
nodes
common
carotid artery
internal
jugular vein
pretracheal
nodes
superior
vena cava
clavicular
nodes

axillary
artery
axillary
vein
axillary
lymph nodes

inguinal
nodes
femoral
artery
femoral
vein

popliteal
fossa nodes
popliteal
artery
popliteal
vein

The lymphatic system consists of a
network of lymph nodes and lymphatic
vessels extending throughout the body.
Lymph fluid, derived from blood
circulating through the tissues, passes
along thin-walled lymphatics which drain
centrally from the periphery. Particular
groupings of lymph nodes occur in the
areas depicted above. As enlargement
of these nodes is common in inflammation
and malignant disease, palpation of the
neck, armpit and groin areas is an
important part of clinical
investigation.

*Obstructive changes in the peripheral
circulation of blood usually lead to a
reduction in local skin temperature; these
changes can be measured accurately using
the infrared thermographic camera to
provide a direct readout of the amount of
vessel narrowing (below):*

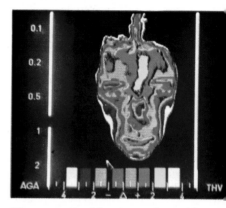

*Thermograph of face in a patient with a
frontal aneurysm.*

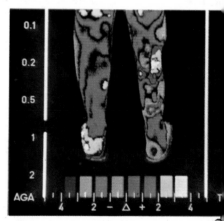

*Thermograph of legs; there is poor flow due
to atherosclerosis on the right.*

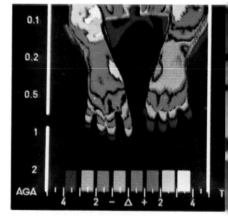

*Thermograph of hands; on the right there
is a noticeable disturbance of blood supply.*

he endocrine system

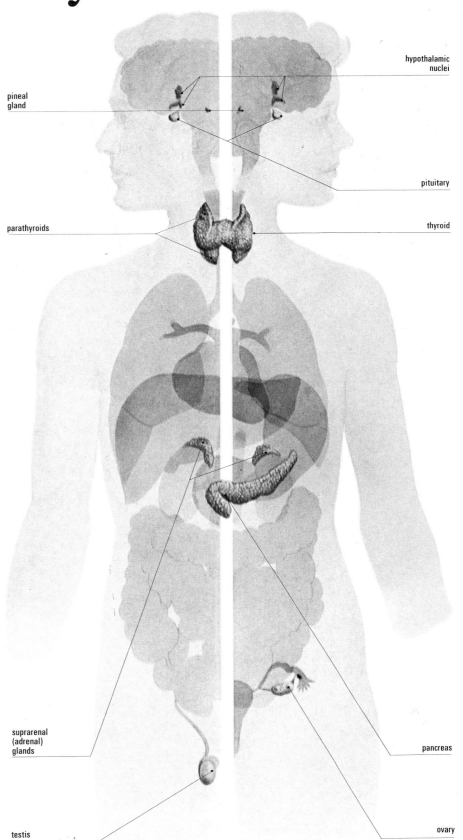

e endocrine glands are ductless struc-
es whose secretions (hormones) pass
ectly into the circulation; hormones in-
ence the activity of specific target
sues elsewhere in the body. There is
distinct and generally harmonious
ationship between the various endo-
ne elements, whether they are separate
gans (eg thyroid and parathyroids) or
cretory cells lodged in other glands (eg
ets of Langerhans in the pancreas). The
ain endocrine structures are shown in
e male and female half diagrams (right).
ntrol of the thyroid, adrenal cortex and
nads is mediated by the trophic hor-
ones of the pituitary. The secretion of
ese is further controlled by the hypo-
alamus to which the pituitary (or 'hypo-
ysis cerebri') is structurally linked. The
pothalamus acts as integrator of the
nctions of the endocrine and nervous
stems. It has direct nervous connec-
ons to the cerebral cortex above and the
sterior part of the pituitary below, and a
nous portal system linking it to the
terior pituitary; it also functions as part
the autonomic system (p. 62). Thus,
hile the main control of hormonal secre-
on is based on a 'feedback' system
here an increased level of hormone in
e blood has a depressant effect on its
wn production), hypothalamic releasing
ctors responding to nervous stimuli can
pidly readjust this state of equilibrium.
his form of control allows the human
dy to cope with the normal stresses of
e in a smooth and co-ordinated fashion.
evertheless, despite its apparent
mplication, the degree of control is pre-
se. Pituitary activity will be discussed in
ore detail in the next section, but in sum-
ary the hypothalamic/hypophyseal axis
as a controlling interest in growth, sexual
ctivity, thyroid function, lactation, water
alance, and carbohydrate, protein and fat
etabolism. The medulla of the adrenal
uprarenal) glands is also centrally con-
olled by the hypothalamus. Epinephrine
nd norepinephrine release places the body
the best possible condition for 'fight or
ight'; in addition to direct effects on the
eart, lungs and skeletal muscle, the blood
ugar level is also increased in order to
rovide extra fuel for burning. More
etailed analysis of these changes allows
me understanding how anxiety and
ress can cause physical disease; exces-
ve pituitary stimulation induced by
igher nervous centers over a long period
an result in damage to the cardio-
ascular system. The parathyroids are
mall, usually four in number, and
lthough embedded in the posterior aspect
f the thyroid gland, have a completely
ifferent function in regulating plasma
alcium and phosphorus levels. With the
ymus and pineal glands they are shown
more detail on p. 50.

hypothalamic
nuclei

pineal
gland

pituitary

parathyroids

thyroid

suprarenal
(adrenal)
glands

pancreas

testis

ovary

pituitary

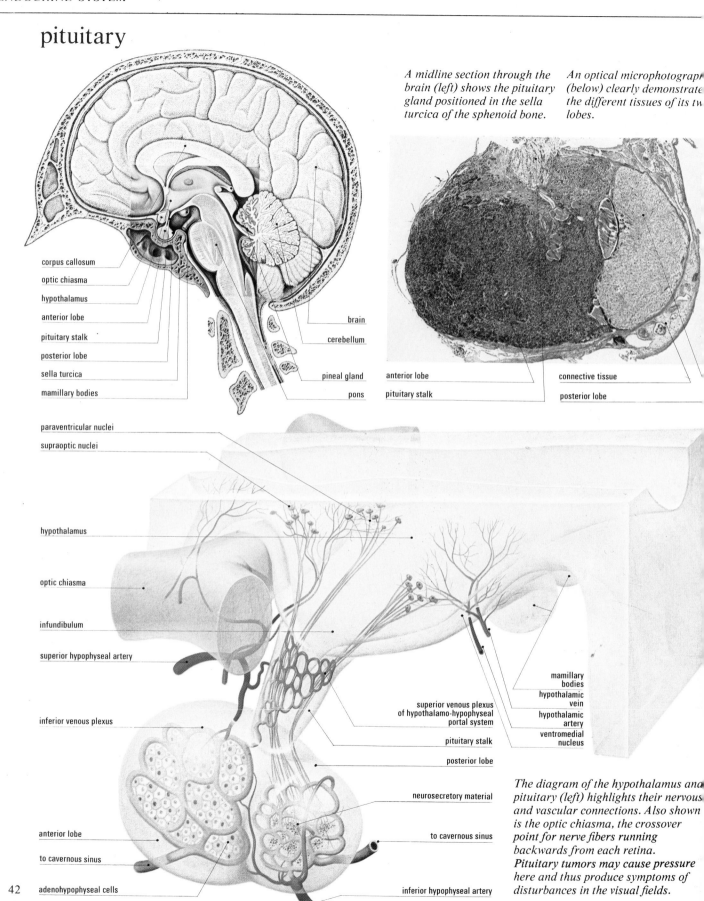

A midline section through the brain (left) shows the pituitary gland positioned in the sella turcica of the sphenoid bone.

An optical microphotograph (below) clearly demonstrates the different tissues of its two lobes.

corpus callosum

optic chiasma

hypothalamus

anterior lobe

pituitary stalk

posterior lobe

sella turcica

mamillary bodies

brain

cerebellum

pineal gland

pons

anterior lobe

pituitary stalk

connective tissue

posterior lobe

paraventricular nuclei

supraoptic nuclei

hypothalamus

optic chiasma

infundibulum

superior hypophyseal artery

inferior venous plexus

anterior lobe

to cavernous sinus

adenohypophyseal cells

mamillary bodies

hypothalamic vein

hypothalamic artery

ventromedial nucleus

superior venous plexus of hypothalamo-hypophyseal portal system

pituitary stalk

posterior lobe

neurosecretory material

to cavernous sinus

inferior hypophyseal artery

The diagram of the hypothalamus and pituitary (left) highlights their nervous and vascular connections. Also shown is the optic chiasma, the crossover point for nerve fibers running backwards from each retina. Pituitary tumors may cause pressure here and thus produce symptoms of disturbances in the visual fields.

classic terms the hypophysis cerebri is
vided into the adenohypophysis and the
urohypophysis. The two parts differ
nsiderably in the type of cells that
ey contain as well as in the details of
eir nerve and blood supplies. The
terior lobe (adenohypophysis) produces
least seven distinct hormones: growth
rmone (GH) controlling prepubertal
velopment; adrenocorticotrophin
CTH) which affects the adrenal cortex;
yrotrophin (TSH) to stimulate thyroid
tivity; prolactin (LTH) which
tivates the lacteal systems of the breast
pregnancy; follicle (FSH) and
terstitial cell (ICSH) stimulating
rmones controlling spermatogenesis/
genesis and androgen/progesterone
cretion in males and females
spectively; and melanocyte (MSH)
imulating hormone which affects skin
gmentation. The two main cell types of
is lobe differ in their reaction to staining
chromophilic or chromophobic.

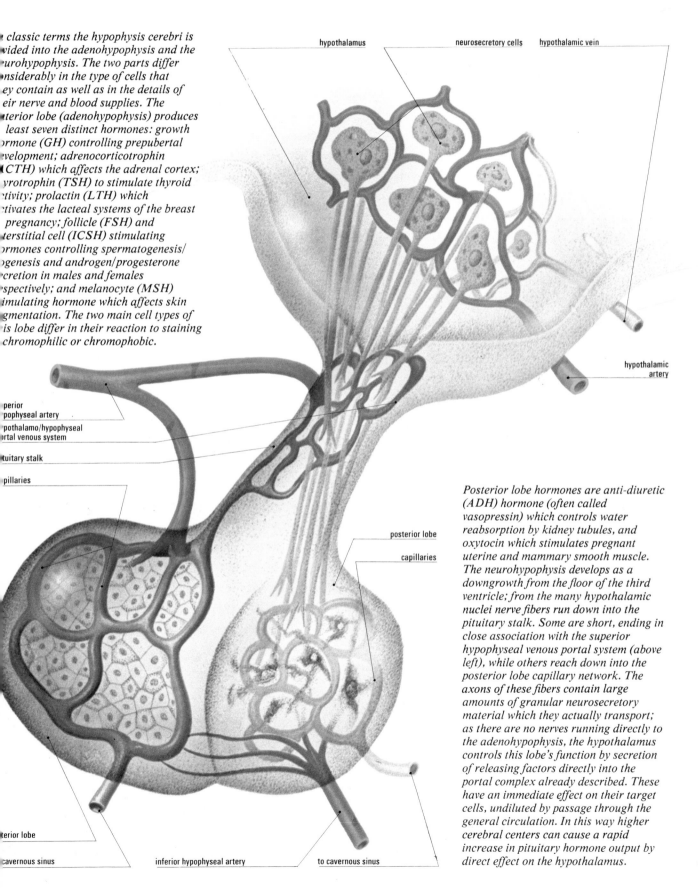

hypothalamus neurosecretory cells hypothalamic vein

hypothalamic artery

perior
pophyseal artery

pothalamo/hypophyseal
rtal venous system

ituitary stalk

pillaries

posterior lobe

capillaries

terior lobe

cavernous sinus inferior hypophyseal artery to cavernous sinus

Posterior lobe hormones are anti-diuretic
(ADH) hormone (often called
vasopressin) which controls water
reabsorption by kidney tubules, and
oxytocin which stimulates pregnant
uterine and mammary smooth muscle.
The neurohypophysis develops as a
downgrowth from the floor of the third
ventricle; from the many hypothalamic
nuclei nerve fibers run down into the
pituitary stalk. Some are short, ending in
close association with the superior
hypophyseal venous portal system (above
left), while others reach down into the
posterior lobe capillary network. The
axons of these fibers contain large
amounts of granular neurosecretory
material which they actually transport;
as there are no nerves running directly to
the adenohypophysis, the hypothalamus
controls this lobe's function by secretion
of releasing factors directly into the
portal complex already described. These
have an immediate effect on their target
cells, undiluted by passage through the
general circulation. In this way higher
cerebral centers can cause a rapid
increase in pituitary hormone output by
direct effect on the hypothalamus.

43

thyroid

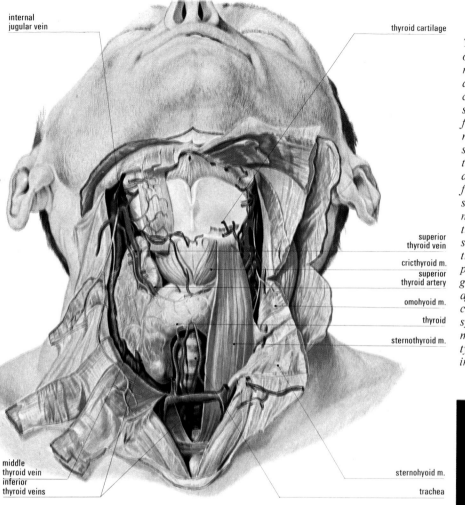

internal
jugular vein

thyroid cartilage

superior
thyroid vein

cricthyroid m.

superior
thyroid artery

omohyoid m.

thyroid

sternothyroid m.

middle
thyroid vein
inferior
thyroid veins

sternohyoid m.

trachea

The thyroid gland is a highly vascular organ situated in the anterior part of the neck (left), consisting of two lobes linked an isthmus; it has a thin capsule of connective tissue which divides the secretory cells into large numbers of follicles (below left) containing an iodine rich colloid material. There are also a smaller number of parafollicular cells; these secrete calcitonin which opposes th actions of parathyroid hormone. Thyrox from the follicular cells, has a powerful stimulant effect on cellular rates of metabolism. An excessive output results the clinical state of thyrotoxicosis – war skin, staring eyes, high pulse rate and tremor. This may be associated (facing page, below) with a thyroid swelling, or goiter. Low thyroid activity after birth m affect brain development and cause cretinism; in the adult the clinical syndrome of low thyroid output is called myxedema. The thermographs show two types of goiter; toxic, with a diffuse increase in vascularity, and nodular.

colloid

follicle

connective tissue

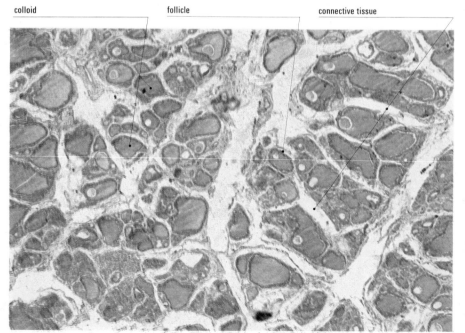

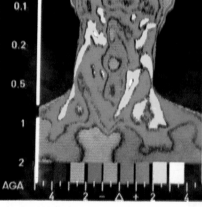

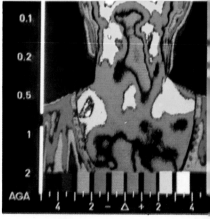

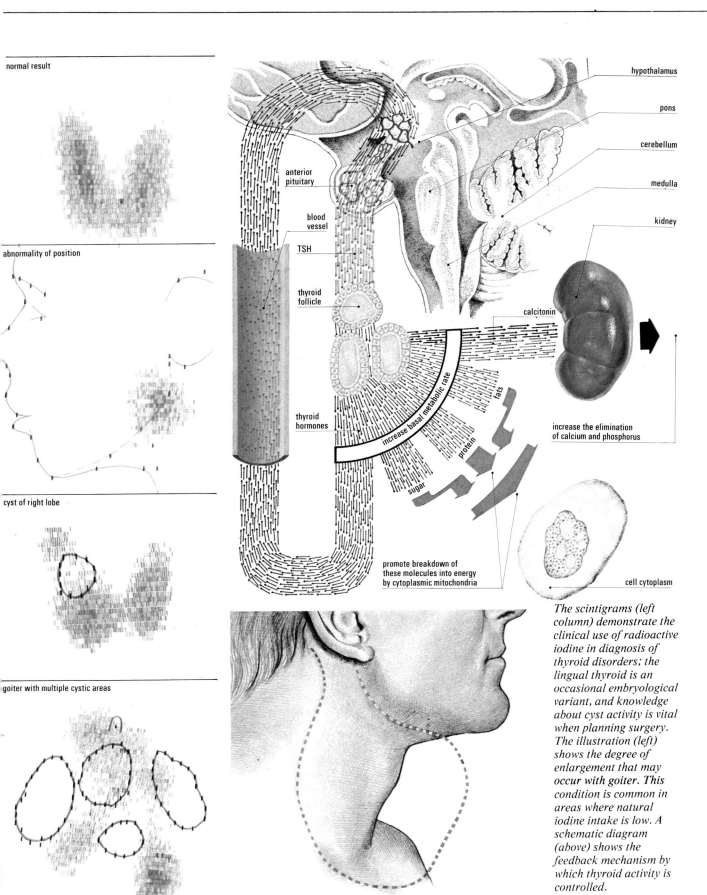

normal result

abnormality of position

cyst of right lobe

goiter with multiple cystic areas

hypothalamus

pons

cerebellum

medulla

kidney

anterior pituitary

blood vessel

TSH

thyroid follicle

thyroid hormones

calcitonin

increase basal metabolic rate

fats

protein

sugar

increase the elimination of calcium and phosphorus

promote breakdown of these molecules into energy by cytoplasmic mitochondria

cell cytoplasm

The scintigrams (left column) demonstrate the clinical use of radioactive iodine in diagnosis of thyroid disorders; the lingual thyroid is an occasional embryological variant, and knowledge about cyst activity is vital when planning surgery. The illustration (left) shows the degree of enlargement that may occur with goiter. This condition is common in areas where natural iodine intake is low. A schematic diagram (above) shows the feedback mechanism by which thyroid activity is controlled.

45

pancreas

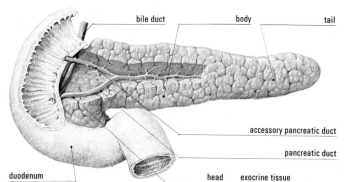

bile duct · body · tail

accessory pancreatic duct

pancreatic duct

duodenum · head

The pancreas is an abdominal gland with both exocrine and endocrine components. The exocrine secretion, pancreatic juice, is rich in starch, fat and protein splitting enzymes which are mixed with bile and aid digestion in the duodenum (left, and p. 88). Scattered throughout the pancreas are small cell clusters of different appearance; the endocrine alpha and beta cells of the islets of Langerhans (below) which produce glucagon and insulin respectively. These hormones are involved in carbohydrate metabolism. A CAT scan (below left) shows the head of the pancreas overlying a vertebral body.

exocrine tissue · islet of Langerhans · excretory ductule

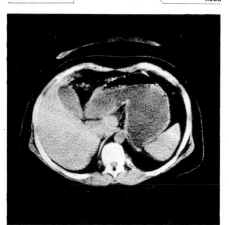

Insulin has a profound effect on metabolism (diagram right): it increases cell membrane permeability to glucose; storage of glucose, after phosphorylation, as glycogen in liver and muscle; oxidation by glycolysis, the pentose shunt and Krebs cycle with consequent production of energy stored as ATP; and glycerolysis with conversion into fatty acids. Insulin also encourages amino acid incorporation into tissue protein. Failure of insulin secretion results in diabetes mellitus, with high blood sugar levels and disturbed metabolism. The blood glucose level is very precisely regulated since glucose is the only energy source that the brain is capable of utilizing.

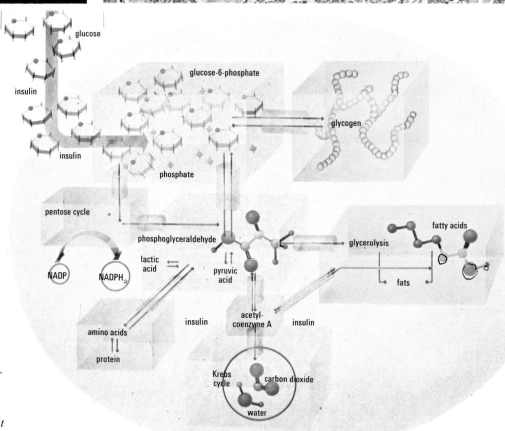

glucose

insulin

insulin

glucose-6-phosphate

glycogen

phosphate

pentose cycle

phosphoglyceraldehyde

glycerolysis

fatty acids

NADP · NADPH$_2$

lactic acid

pyruvic acid

fats

amino acids

insulin

acetyl-coenzyme A

insulin

protein

Krebs cycle

carbon dioxide

water

adrenals

stomach

inferior vena cava

right adrenal gland

left adrenal gland

abdominal aorta

left kidney

These paired glands lie against the upper poles of the kidneys; each consists of a cortex and medulla (below left) with the cortex further subdivided into three layers. The main cortical hormone groups are: glucocorticoids, eg. cortisol which affects carbohydrate metabolism; mineralocorticoids, like aldosterone which causes sodium retention in the renal tubules, and the sex hormones, androgens and estrogens, which influence secondary sexual characteristics. As a result of sympathetic stimulation (p. 62) the chromaffin cells of the adrenal medulla release epinephrine and norepinephrine in large quantities during episodes of fear, stress or danger.

capsule

cortex

zona glomerulosa

connective tissue capsule

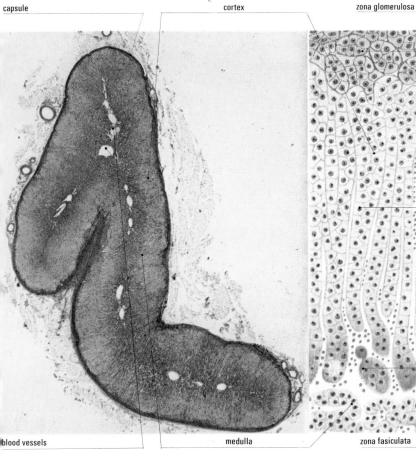

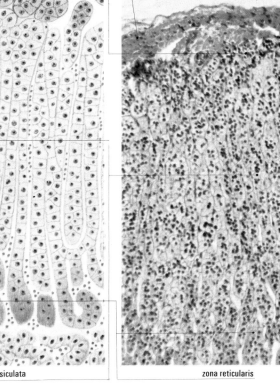

blood vessels

medulla

zona fasiculata

zona reticularis

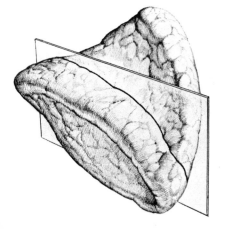

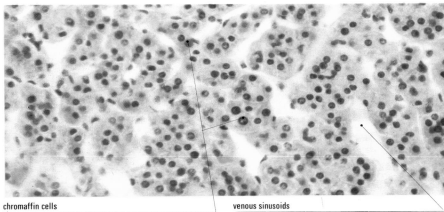

chromaffin cells

venous sinusoids

testes

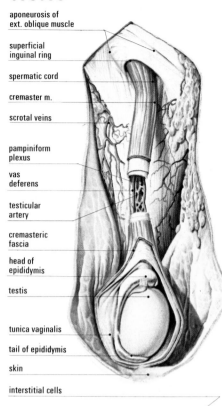

aponeurosis of
ext. oblique muscle

superficial
inguinal ring

spermatic cord

cremaster m.

scrotal veins

pampiniform
plexus

vas
deferens

testicular
artery

cremasteric
fascia

head of
epididymis

testis

tunica vaginalis

tail of epididymis

skin

interstitial cells

germinal cells (spermatogonia)
connective
tissue septum

seminiferous tubule

Although developed intra-abdominally, the reproductive glands of the male are suspended extra-abdominally by the scrotum (left) and spermatic cords. Within each testis are several hundred convoluted seminiferous tubules which drain via the epididymis to the vas deferens. Spermatogenesis, the development of spermatozoa, takes place (below left) within the tubules; their fertility depends on testicular temperature being lower than the body's. The vasa deferentia carry the spermatozoa to the seminal vesicles at the base of the bladder. Lying between the tubules are the interstitial (Leydig and Sertoli) cells which produce testosterone under anterior pituitary control (ICSH and FSH). Testosterone and other cortical androgens (below) stimulate testicular descent during fetal development, growth of the external reproductive organs, and masculinization, the appearance of male secondary sexual characteristics.

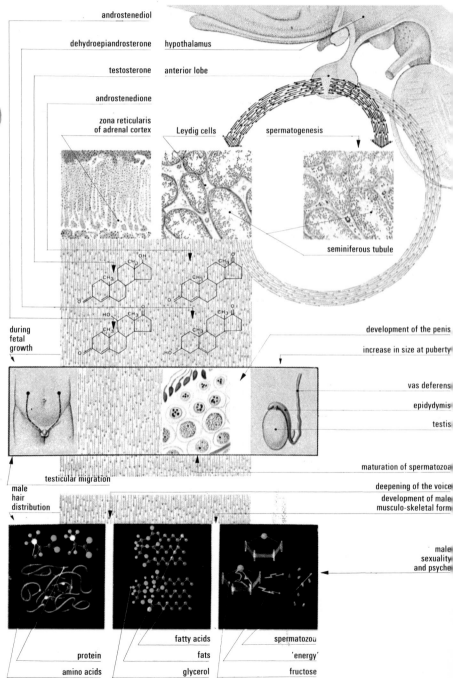

androstenediol

dehydroepiandrosterone

testosterone

androstenedione

zona reticularis
of adrenal cortex

hypothalamus

anterior lobe

Leydig cells

spermatogenesis

seminiferous tubule

during
fetal
growth

testicular migration

male
hair
distribution

development of the penis

increase in size at puberty

vas deferens

epidydymis

testis

maturation of spermatozoa

deepening of the voice

development of male
musculo-skeletal form

male
sexuality
and psyche

protein

amino acids

fatty acids

fats

glycerol

spermatozoa

'energy'

fructose

ovaries

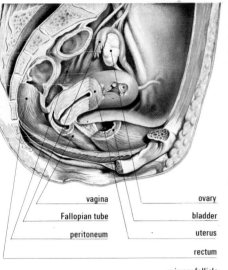

A sagittal section through the female pelvis (left) shows the Fallopian tube closely applied to the ovary, which is suspended by a fold of peritoneum – the ovarian ligament. The ovaries are homologous with the testes of the male. Each has a cortex rich in follicles (below left) which contain the primordial germ cells or oocytes; under hormonal control one of these follicles matures at each menstrual cycle (below) and ruptures into the peritoneal cavity. The released ovum passes into the Fallopian tube, ready for fertilization, while the follicle lining forms the corpus luteum. This becomes greatly enlarged if implantation of a fertilized ovum occurs; if not, then it degenerates into a form of scar tissue, the corpus albicans, and the menstrual cycle begins again.

vagina
Fallopian tube
peritoneum

ovary
bladder
uterus
rectum
primary follicle

mature follicle

nucleus

zona pellucida

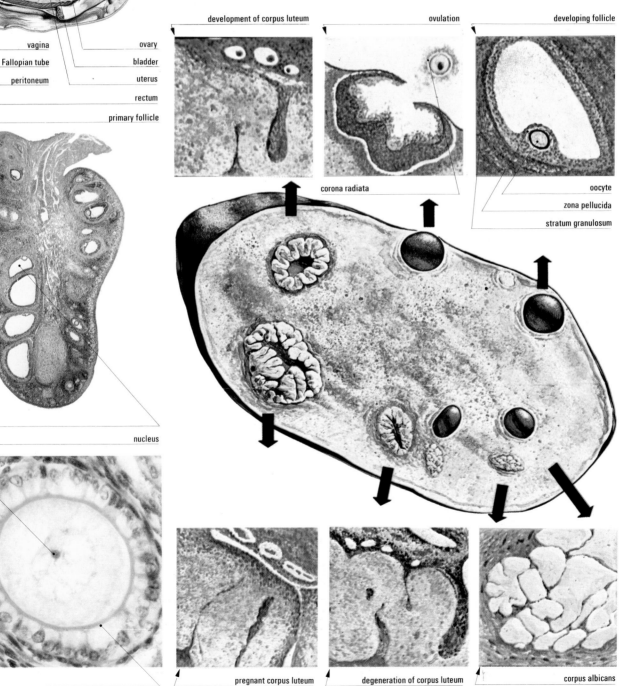

development of corpus luteum

ovulation

developing follicle

corona radiata

oocyte
zona pellucida
stratum granulosum

pregnant corpus luteum

degeneration of corpus luteum

corpus albicans

49

parathyroids

The parathyroids are four small ovoid structures embedded in the posterior aspect of the thyroid lobes (diagram below). They receive a rich blood supply from the inferior thyroid artery and are vitally concerned with the regulation of blood calcium levels, by secretion of parathormone which acts in opposition to calcitonin (p. 44).

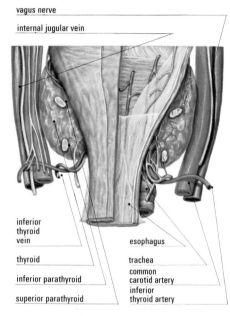

vagus nerve

internal jugular vein

inferior thyroid vein

thyroid

inferior parathyroid

superior parathyroid

esophagus

trachea

common carotid artery

inferior thyroid artery

The regulation of calcium and phosphorus blood levels depends (below) on dietary intake, the mineral reserves of the skeletal system, and the excretion rates in the kidney. Excessive parathormone secretion leads to bone demineralization and high urine calcium levels.

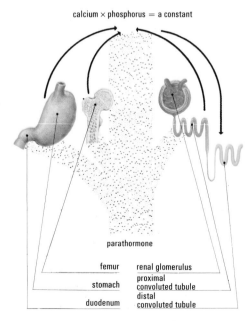

calcium × phosphorus = a constant

parathormone

femur

stomach

duodenum

renal glomerulus

proximal convoluted tubule

distal convoluted tubule

pineal

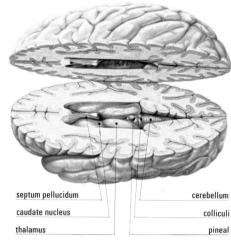

septum pellucidum

caudate nucleus

thalamus

cerebellum

colliculi

pineal

The pineal gland is a small pea-shaped cerebral structure which is closely related to the floor of the third ventricle (above). It has a rich blood supply, but often calcifies in later life, providing a useful marker for radiologists.

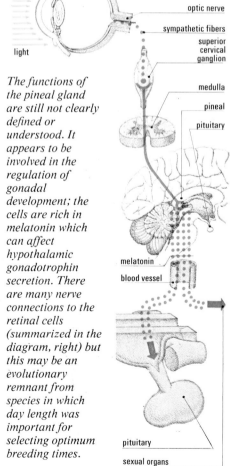

retina

optic nerve

sympathetic fibers

superior cervical ganglion

light

medulla

pineal

pituitary

melatonin

blood vessel

pituitary

sexual organs

The functions of the pineal gland are still not clearly defined or understood. It appears to be involved in the regulation of gonadal development; the cells are rich in melatonin which can affect hypothalamic gonadotrophin secretion. There are many nerve connections to the retinal cells (summarized in the diagram, right) but this may be an evolutionary remnant from species in which day length was important for selecting optimum breeding times.

thymus

The thymus varies in size with age, and after puberty gradually atrophies in the retrosternal space (below). It has a lobular structure rich in lymphocytes and reticular cells. Knowledge of thymic function is not yet complete, but it appears to be vital in ensuring normal development of lymphoid tissues as well as the establishment of a competent cellular immunity system.

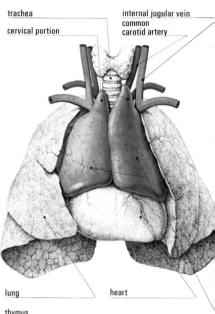

trachea

cervical portion

internal jugular vein

common carotid artery

lung

thymus

heart

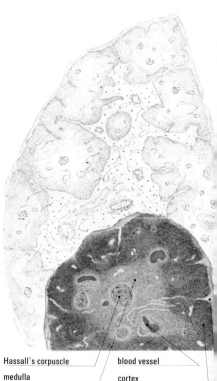

Hassall's corpuscle

medulla

fibrous capsule

blood vessel

cortex

he nervous system

he human nervous system is the final
esult of millions of years of evolution.
Man's predominance in the order of living
pecies is due entirely to the complexity
nd versatility of this system which, al-
hough deeply investigated by re-
earchers, is still poorly understood. Its
tructure and activities are inseparable
rom every aspect of our daily lives
whether physical, intellectual or cultural;
he millions upon millions of cells inter-
mesh via a myriad of connecting pathways to provide functions varying from
he abstract appreciation of literature and
music to the calculated fury of war.
Despite recent huge advances in micro-
rocessor technology the brain is still the
most versatile computer known to man,
et its vast complexity requires less power
o run than a small electric light bulb. In
ssence the nervous system has two re-
ponsibilities; maintenance of structural
ntegrity by homeostatic control of the in-
ernal environment, and adaptation to
hanging external circumstances. All
ving organisms exhibit these qualities to a
esser degree, but the human nervous
ystem has refined them to an unparal-
led pitch. For instance, a particular
timulus pattern can be compared with
imilar patterns stored in a memory; as
many potential responses exist to the chal-
enge, a selection is made based on ex-
erience. The appropriate response is
made and then re-assessed in the light of
he consequences. If effective, both the
ecision and the reasoning behind it are
tored in the memory, ie. the brain 'learns'.
This process has been highly refined in the
uman brain so that the decision taking
an be based on abstract reasoning rather
han personal experience. In addition, a
ast amount of sensory information is
onstantly transmitted to the brain from
eripheral receptors, whether specialized
ense organs (which are described in more
etail in the next section) or simply modi-
ied nerve endings. This information is
hared in the complex interconnections of
he central neurons and an appropriate
attern of response determined. Suitable
orders' to effector cells then emerge along
he efferent (motor) nerves. Most of this
circuitry is reflex and automatic, although
cope exists for modification by higher
centres. Examination of the brain shows
hree distinct divisions which have struc-
ural counterparts in the story of verte-
orate evolution. Ascending from the spinal
cord, and contained entirely within the
rigid protective box of the skull are the
hindbrain, midbrain and forebrain (rhom-
encephalon, mesencephalon and prosen-
cephalon respectively). The forebrain is
urther divided into cerebrum (telen-
cephalon) and its thalamic and hypothalamic connections (diencephalon). The
hindbrain consists of the medulla oblongata, pons and cerebellum. Together with
he midbrain, the pons and medulla are
known collectively as the brainstem.

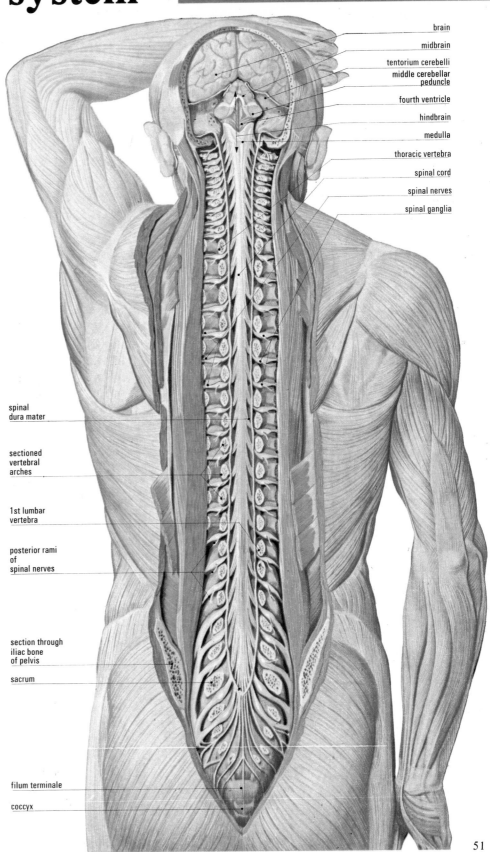

brain
midbrain
tentorium cerebelli
middle cerebellar
peduncle
fourth ventricle
hindbrain
medulla
thoracic vertebra
spinal cord
spinal nerves
spinal ganglia

spinal
dura mater

sectioned
vertebral
arches

1st lumbar
vertebra

posterior rami
of
spinal nerves

section through
iliac bone
of pelvis

sacrum

filum terminale

coccyx

51

The neuron (right, impregnated with a silver stain) is the basic excitable cell unit of the nervous system. Neurons display wide variation in shape and size; generally they have a large number of dendritic (afferent, or sensory) processes but a single axonal (efferent, or motor) extension. Axons may be very long, and the diagrams (below) show how bundles of axons, named tracts, make up the 'white matter' that surrounds the 'grey matter' of spinal nerve cells. The diagrams have been greatly simplified, but show (left) a typical motor pathway from cortical cells to the muscles of the head, trunk and limbs, and (right) a sensory circuit. Note how in both cases fibers decussate (cross) to the opposite side.

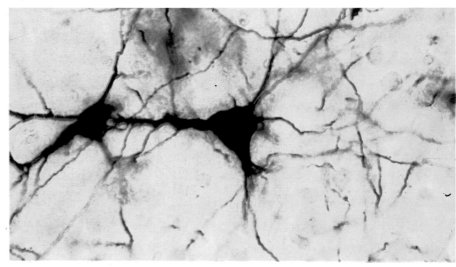

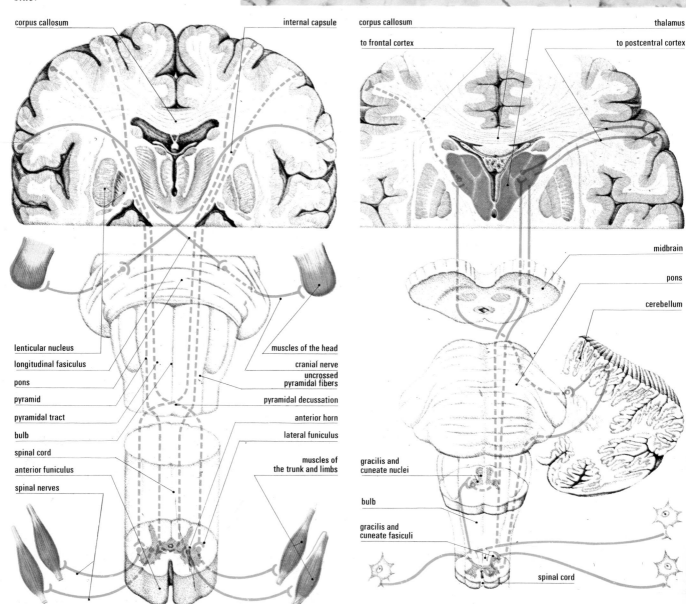

corpus callosum

internal capsule

corpus callosum

thalamus

to frontal cortex

to postcentral cortex

midbrain

pons

cerebellum

lenticular nucleus

longitudinal fasiculus

pons

pyramid

pyramidal tract

bulb

spinal cord

anterior funiculus

spinal nerves

muscles of the head

cranial nerve

uncrossed
pyramidal fibers

pyramidal decussation

anterior horn

lateral funiculus

muscles of
the trunk and limbs

gracilis and
cuneate nuclei

bulb

gracilis and
cuneate fasiculi

spinal cord

nlike the larger number of ·inal nerves, the twelve pairs of ranial nerves are directly ontinuous with the brain. Their ·otor and sensory nuclei are ·ainly grouped together in the ·rain stem and are shown ·iagram below right) in red ·nd yellow respectively. The

sequence, from above below, is: III oculomotor; IV trochlear; V trigeminal; VI abducent; VII facial; VIII vestibulo-cochlear; IX glossopharyngeal; X vagus; XI accessory and XII hypoglossal. The olfactory (I) nerve (above right) transmits sensory impulses directly to the olfactory bulb beneath the frontal lobe; the optic (II) nerve runs back from the retina to the visual cortex of the occipital lobe. The motor and sensory functions of the other cranial nerves are shown in diagrammatic form (below).

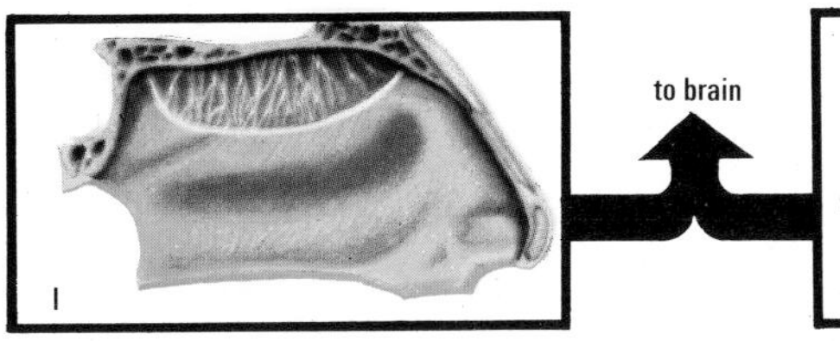

to brain

I

II

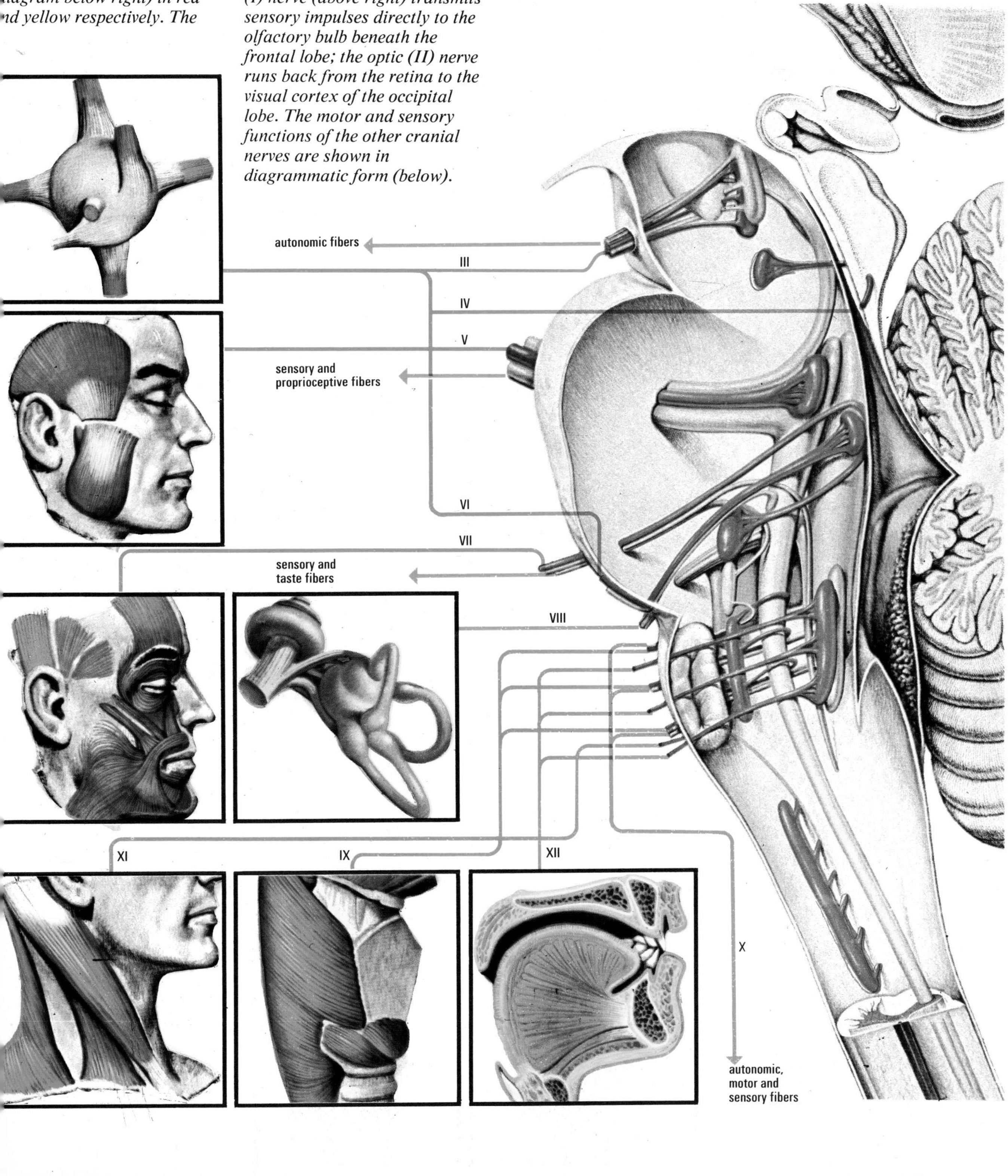

autonomic fibers ←

III

IV

V

sensory and
proprioceptive fibers ←

VI

VII

sensory and
taste fibers ←

VIII

XI

IX

XII

X

autonomic,
motor and
sensory fibers

53

central nervous system

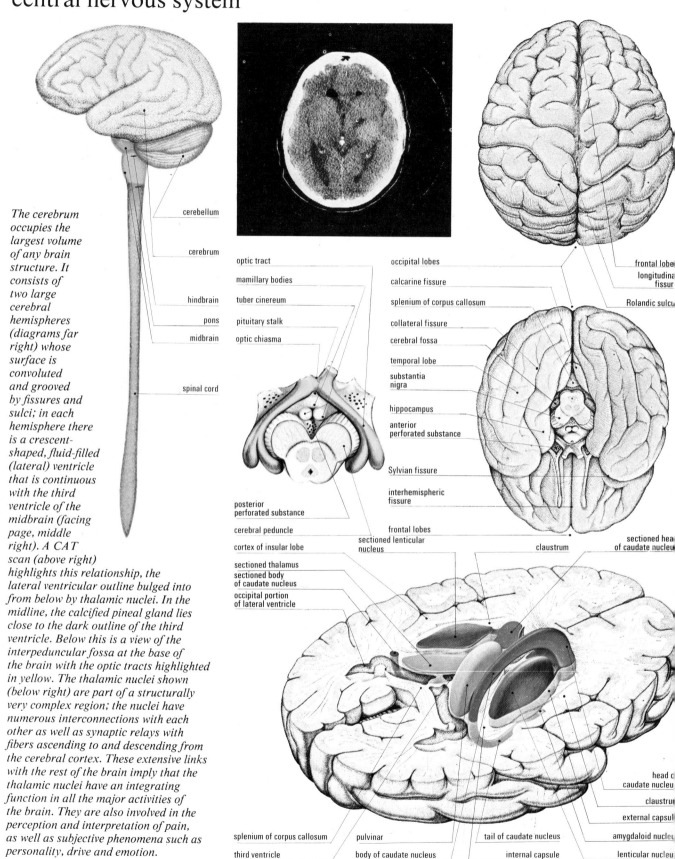

The cerebrum occupies the largest volume of any brain structure. It consists of two large cerebral hemispheres (diagrams far right) whose surface is convoluted and grooved by fissures and sulci; in each hemisphere there is a crescent-shaped, fluid-filled (lateral) ventricle that is continuous with the third ventricle of the midbrain (facing page, middle right). A CAT scan (above right) highlights this relationship, the lateral ventricular outline bulged into from below by thalamic nuclei. In the midline, the calcified pineal gland lies close to the dark outline of the third ventricle. Below this is a view of the interpeduncular fossa at the base of the brain with the optic tracts highlighted in yellow. The thalamic nuclei shown (below right) are part of a structurally very complex region; the nuclei have numerous interconnections with each other as well as synaptic relays with fibers ascending to and descending from the cerebral cortex. These extensive links with the rest of the brain imply that the thalamic nuclei have an integrating function in all the major activities of the brain. They are also involved in the perception and interpretation of pain, as well as subjective phenomena such as personality, drive and emotion.

cerebellum

cerebrum

hindbrain

pons

midbrain

spinal cord

optic tract

mamillary bodies

tuber cinereum

pituitary stalk

optic chiasma

posterior perforated substance

cerebral peduncle

cortex of insular lobe

occipital lobes

calcarine fissure

splenium of corpus callosum

collateral fissure

cerebral fossa

temporal lobe

substantia nigra

hippocampus

anterior perforated substance

Sylvian fissure

interhemispheric fissure

frontal lobes

frontal lobe

longitudinal fissur

Rolandic sulcu

sectioned lenticular nucleus

claustrum

sectioned hea of caudate nucleu

sectioned thalamus

sectioned body of caudate nucleus

occipital portion of lateral ventricle

head o caudate nucleu

claustrum

external capsul

amygdaloid nuclei

lenticular nuclei

splenium of corpus callosum

pulvinar

tail of caudate nucleus

third ventricle

body of caudate nucleus

internal capsule

54

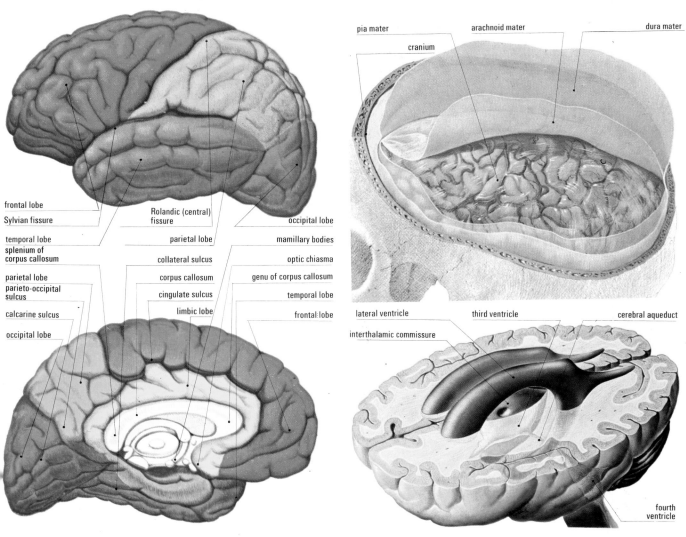

pia mater   arachnoid mater   dura mater

cranium

frontal lobe

Sylvian fissure

Rolandic (central) fissure

occipital lobe

temporal lobe

splenium of corpus callosum

parietal lobe

mamillary bodies

parietal lobe

collateral sulcus

optic chiasma

parieto-occipital sulcus

corpus callosum

genu of corpus callosum

cingulate sulcus

temporal lobe

calcarine sulcus

limbic lobe

frontal lobe

occipital lobe

lateral ventricle   third ventricle   cerebral aqueduct

interthalamic commissure

fourth ventricle

The cerebral cortex is shown (diagrams above) from both lateral and medial aspects. The innermost of the meningeal layers, the pia mater, is very thin but rich in blood vessels (above right). Stimulation of different parts of the cerebral cortex (below left) has shown the predominant functions of each area; the 'motor homunculus' (below right) displays the large number of cortical cells required for fine movements of the hand and fingers as well as for vocal sounds such as talking or singing.

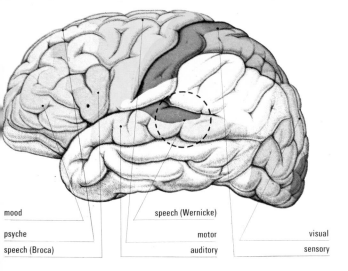

mood

psyche

speech (Broca)

speech (Wernicke)

motor

auditory

visual

sensory

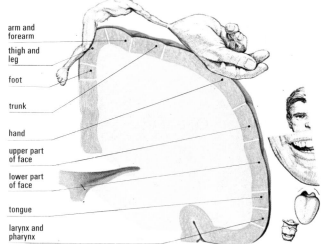

arm and forearm

thigh and leg

foot

trunk

hand

upper part of face

lower part of face

tongue

larynx and pharynx

55

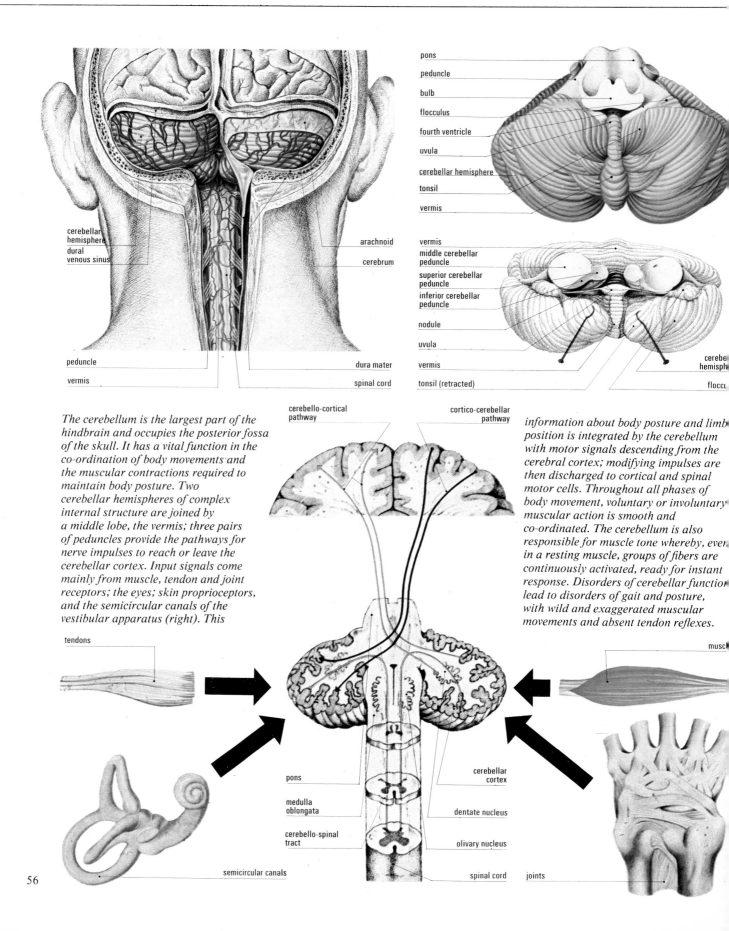

pons
peduncle
bulb
flocculus
fourth ventricle
uvula
cerebellar hemisphere
tonsil
vermis

vermis
middle cerebellar peduncle
superior cerebellar peduncle
inferior cerebellar peduncle
nodule
uvula
vermis
tonsil (retracted)

cerebe
hemisph

flocc

cerebellar hemisphere
dural venous sinus

arachnoid
cerebrum

peduncle
vermis

dura mater
spinal cord

The cerebellum is the largest part of the hindbrain and occupies the posterior fossa of the skull. It has a vital function in the co-ordination of body movements and the muscular contractions required to maintain body posture. Two cerebellar hemispheres of complex internal structure are joined by a middle lobe, the vermis; three pairs of peduncles provide the pathways for nerve impulses to reach or leave the cerebellar cortex. Input signals come mainly from muscle, tendon and joint receptors; the eyes; skin proprioceptors, and the semicircular canals of the vestibular apparatus (right). This

information about body posture and limb position is integrated by the cerebellum with motor signals descending from the cerebral cortex; modifying impulses are then discharged to cortical and spinal motor cells. Throughout all phases of body movement, voluntary or involuntary muscular action is smooth and co-ordinated. The cerebellum is also responsible for muscle tone whereby, even in a resting muscle, groups of fibers are continuously activated, ready for instant response. Disorders of cerebellar function lead to disorders of gait and posture, with wild and exaggerated muscular movements and absent tendon reflexes.

cerebello-cortical pathway
cortico-cerebellar pathway

tendons

musc

pons
medulla oblongata
cerebello-spinal tract

cerebellar cortex
dentate nucleus
olivary nucleus

semicircular canals
spinal cord
joints

mediately above the
dulla oblongata the
ainstem expands into the
ns, then continues as the
idbrain. Dorsal to the pons
a tent-shaped recess, the
urth ventricle; this
ructure is lined with
endymal cells and is
ntinuous with the third
ntricle above, via the
rebral aqueduct, and with
e central canal of the
inal medulla below. These
lationships are displayed
a posterior fossa
ssection (below) with a
gment of cerebellum
moved, and in dorsal and
ntral aspects (right). The
idbrain is about 2 cm long
d continues cranially as
e two cerebral peduncles

on the ventral aspect;
dorsally, the tectum expands
into two pairs of colliculi,
which are involved in visual
and auditory reflex
pathways. The cranial
nerves whose nuclei are
arranged throughout the
pons and midbrain (p. 53)
emerge at various levels.
Scattered throughout these
brainstem nuclei and fiber
bundles are networks of grey
and white matter known as
the reticular formation. Like
the thalamic nuclei, this
structure has numerous
intra-cerebral connections
considered vital for
locomotor co-ordination,
sleep states and the
autonomic control of
breathing and heart rates.

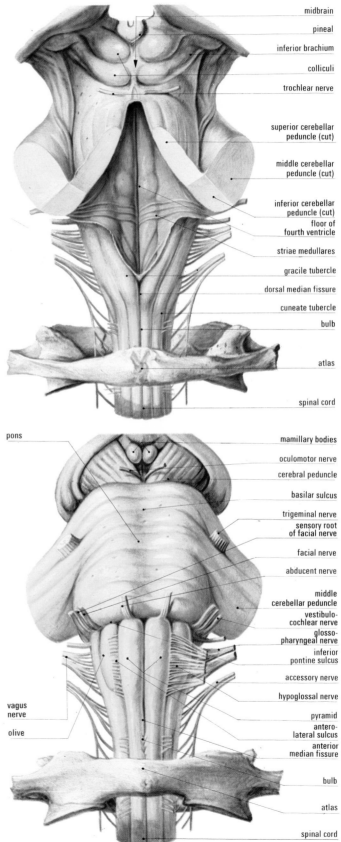

midbrain
pineal
inferior brachium
colliculi
trochlear nerve
superior cerebellar peduncle (cut)
middle cerebellar peduncle (cut)
inferior cerebellar peduncle (cut)
floor of fourth ventricle
striae medullares
gracile tubercle
dorsal median fissure
cuneate tubercle
bulb
atlas
spinal cord

pons
mamillary bodies
oculomotor nerve
cerebral peduncle
basilar sulcus
trigeminal nerve
sensory root of facial nerve
facial nerve
abducent nerve
middle cerebellar peduncle
vestibulo-cochlear nerve
glosso-pharyngeal nerve
inferior pontine sulcus
accessory nerve
hypoglossal nerve
pyramid
antero-lateral sulcus
anterior median fissure
bulb
atlas
vagus nerve
olive
spinal cord

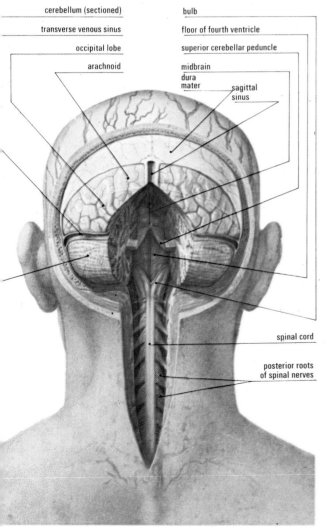

cerebellum (sectioned)
transverse venous sinus
occipital lobe
arachnoid
bulb
floor of fourth ventricle
superior cerebellar peduncle
midbrain
dura mater
sagittal sinus
spinal cord
posterior roots of spinal nerves

The spinal cord is the elongated portion of the central nervous system that occupies the bony canal of the vertebral column (near right). Oval in cross-section, its width decreases as it descends although there are enlargements in the cervical and lumbar regions, each associated with a nerve plexus. Dorsal and ventral roots emerge at intervals (far right) to penetrate the dural coverings and then fuse, forming paired spinal nerves. Below the second lumbar vertebra the spinal cord continues as a fine thread, the filum terminale, which is attached to the coccyx internally. Arranged around the central column of 'grey matter' (below), the spinal cord 'white matter' consists of myelinated fiber bundles; these tracts carry sensory information up to the thalamic and cerebellar nuclei, and motor output downwards from cortical, midbrain and hindbrain nuclei.

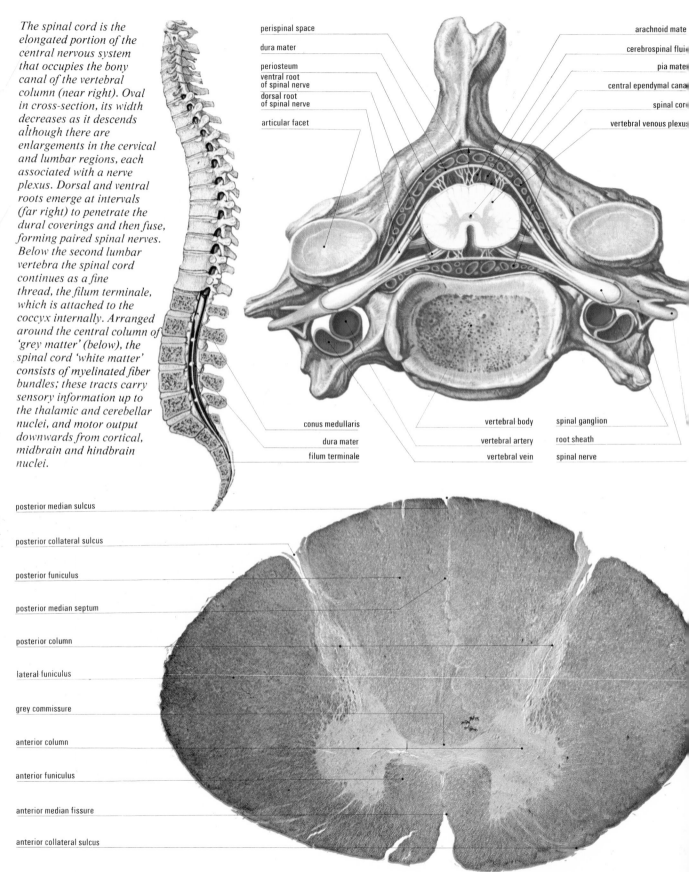

perispinal space

dura mater

periosteum

ventral root of spinal nerve

dorsal root of spinal nerve

articular facet

arachnoid mater

cerebrospinal fluid

pia mater

central ependymal canal

spinal cord

vertebral venous plexus

conus medullaris

dura mater

filum terminale

vertebral body

vertebral artery

vertebral vein

spinal ganglion

root sheath

spinal nerve

posterior median sulcus

posterior collateral sulcus

posterior funiculus

posterior median septum

posterior column

lateral funiculus

grey commissure

anterior column

anterior funiculus

anterior median fissure

anterior collateral sulcus

A frontal section of the brain (below, the plane of section indicated by the smaller diagram) displays the general arrangements of cortical cells and some of the deeper connecting layers. The thermographs (right) show a 'hot' area in the posterior view which was associated with tumor lying just beneath the bony vault of the skull. A thalamic tumor such as the one depicted below is more difficult to localize and requires radioisotope imaging (see over) or CAT scanning.

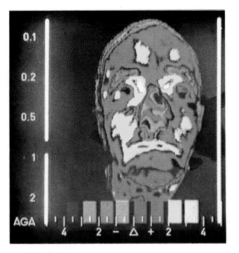

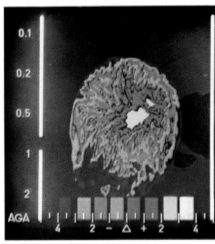

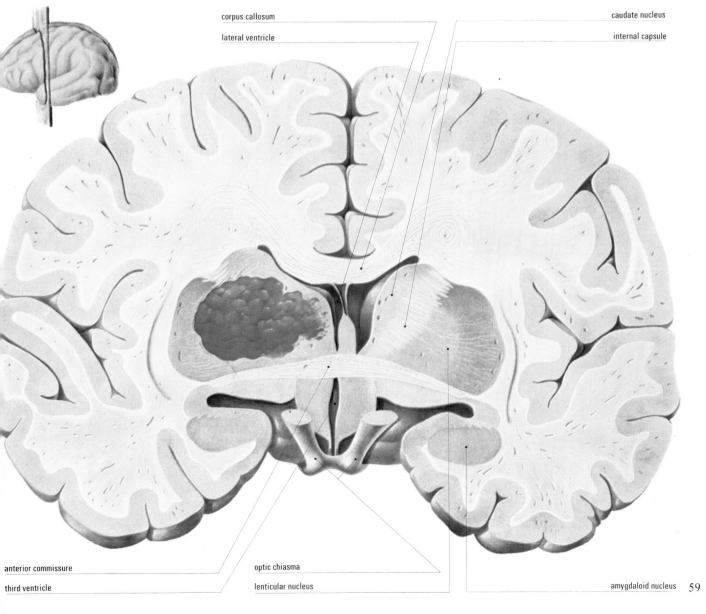

corpus callosum

caudate nucleus

lateral ventricle

internal capsule

anterior commissure

optic chiasma

third ventricle

lenticular nucleus

amygdaloid nucleus 59

The use of nuclear isotopes in clinical investigation has a particular application in the diagnosis of tumors of the brain. Most neuroradiological methods depends on the introduction of contrast medium via lumbar puncture or carotid arteriography. These procedures are invasive, and carry a slight but definite risk. Computer Assisted Tomography (CAT) has minimized this problem considerably, but the scanner equipment is very expensive and therefore localized to a few centers at present. Technetium-99 is an isotope of short half-life which can be used to label substances with a particular affinity for brain tissues; its uptake by a tumor will depend on the latter's size, type and vascularity. The series below shows four scans of a patient's brain after the intravenous injection of Tc-99 tracer. The varying gamma photon emissions are recorded as alterations of line density and color. There is a pathological accumulation of tracer visible in the right temporal lobe, shown in the anterior and right lateral views.

anterior

right lateral

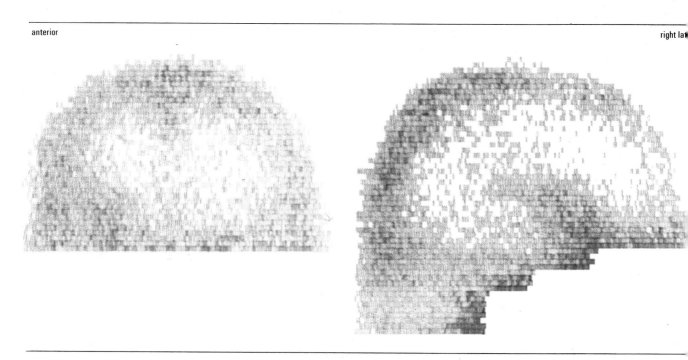

left oblique

posterior

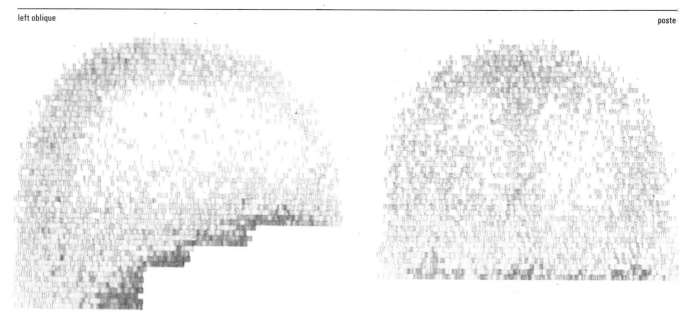

peripheral nervous system

The dorsal rami of the spinal nerves are generally smaller than their ventral counterparts and supply the muscles and skin of the neck and trunk close to the posterior midline. The limbs and the rest of the body are supplied by the ventral rami which also form cervical, lumbar and sacral plexuses.

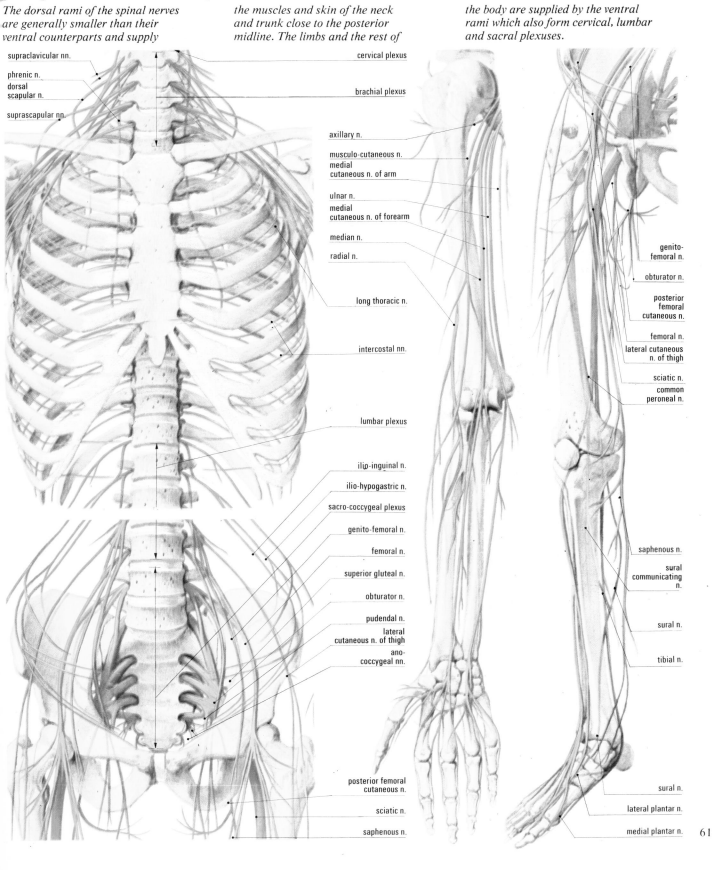

supraclavicular nn.

phrenic n.
dorsal scapular n.

suprascapular nn.

cervical plexus

brachial plexus

axillary n.

musculo-cutaneous n.
medial cutaneous n. of arm

ulnar n.
medial cutaneous n. of forearm

median n.

radial n.

long thoracic n.

intercostal nn.

lumbar plexus

ilio-inguinal n.

ilio-hypogastric n.

sacro-coccygeal plexus

genito-femoral n.

femoral n.

superior gluteal n.

obturator n.

pudendal n.

lateral cutaneous n. of thigh

ano-coccygeal nn.

posterior femoral cutaneous n.

sciatic n.

saphenous n.

genito-femoral n.

obturator n.

posterior femoral cutaneous n.

femoral n.
lateral cutaneous n. of thigh

sciatic n.
common peroneal n.

saphenous n.

sural communicating n.

sural n.

tibial n.

sural n.

lateral plantar n.

medial plantar n.

61

The peripheral nervous system provides a complete network of motor and sensory nerve fibers connecting the central nervous system to the rest of the body. Sharing some of those fiber pathways but separately involved in the control of exocrine glands, blood vessels, viscera and external genitalia, there is an autonomic nervous system. This has two components, sympathetic and parasympathetic, with opposing effects summarised in the illustration (right). There are marked differences in the details of autonomic efferent outflow, but parasympathetic activity is generally localised and associated with the release of acetylcholine, whereas sympathetic responses are more widespread and result from epinephrine and norepinephrine. Unlike the somatic peripheral nerves, the autonomic efferent nerve pathways are interrupted by a peripheral ganglion before innervating the target organ. The sympathetic ganglia are mainly collected into two trunks on each side of the spinal column; parasympathetic outflow in the oculomotor, facial and glossopharyngeal nerves runs via four associated ganglia, while the vagus and pelvic splanchnic nerves relay via minute ganglia in the walls of the individual viscera.

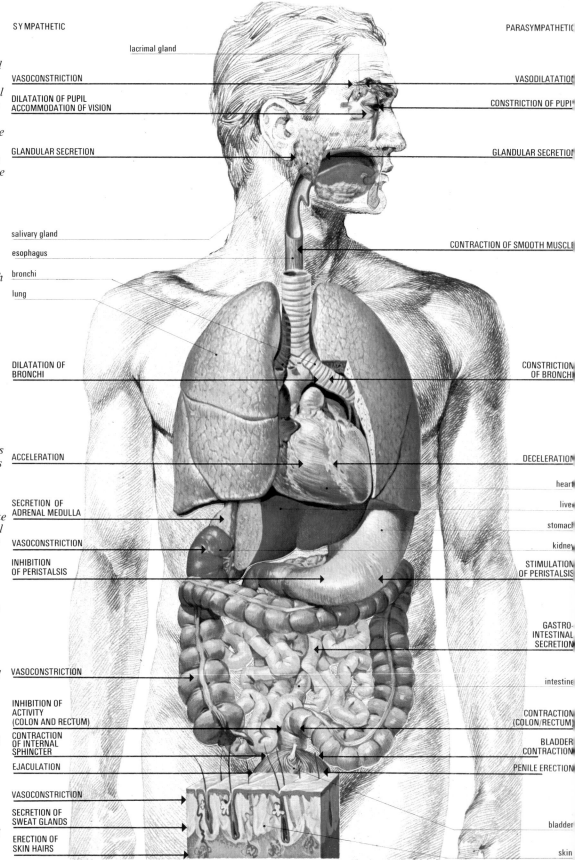

SYMPATHETIC

PARASYMPATHETIC

lacrimal gland

VASOCONSTRICTION

VASODILATATION

DILATATION OF PUPIL
ACCOMMODATION OF VISION

CONSTRICTION OF PUPIL

GLANDULAR SECRETION

GLANDULAR SECRETION

salivary gland

esophagus

bronchi

lung

CONTRACTION OF SMOOTH MUSCLE

DILATATION OF
BRONCHI

CONSTRICTION
OF BRONCHI

ACCELERATION

DECELERATION

heart

SECRETION OF
ADRENAL MEDULLA

liver

stomach

VASOCONSTRICTION

kidney

INHIBITION
OF PERISTALSIS

STIMULATION
OF PERISTALSIS

GASTRO-
INTESTINAL
SECRETION

VASOCONSTRICTION

intestine

INHIBITION OF
ACTIVITY
(COLON AND RECTUM)

CONTRACTION
(COLON/RECTUM)

CONTRACTION
OF INTERNAL
SPHINCTER

BLADDER
CONTRACTION

EJACULATION

PENILE ERECTION

VASOCONSTRICTION

SECRETION OF
SWEAT GLANDS

bladder

ERECTION OF
SKIN HAIRS

skin

the special senses

In the struggle for survival that character-
ises evolution, the animals best able to
employ natural environmental phenomena for hunting or hiding were the
ones that survived. The ability to smell
predator or prey, to hear noise and
identify it with danger, or to use shade as a
refuge were all features that helped in the
never ending conflict. Some evolutionary
advances in the development of the special
sense organs were critical for man's cur-
rent pre-eminence. In man, the physiological functions of sight, smell, taste,
hearing and touch all provide a central

sensory input from highly specialized
receptor cells located in the eyes, nose,
tongue, ears and skin. The electromag-
netic radiation presenting as light in the
visible spectrum is detected by the photo-
receptors of the retina. To make this basic
process more efficient, light energy is
focused by a crystalline lens onto the
retinal surface (p. 66). The number of cells
and their rich central connections allow a
recognisable picture to be formed of the
outside world in which shape and form
can be recognised, as well as movement.
As evolution progressed the location of the

eyes changed from a lateral to a more
anterior position. This meant that the
visual fields overlapped to give binocular
vision which, in man and other primates,
has been further developed to give a
stereoscopic quality with accurate perception of depth and distance, even when the
head is moving. Protected by the bony
structures of the orbit, washed and cleaned
by the lacrimal apparatus and eyelids, the
eyeball has a very precise muscular
control mediated via the cranial nerves; its
basic structural arrangements are displayed in the sectioned view below.

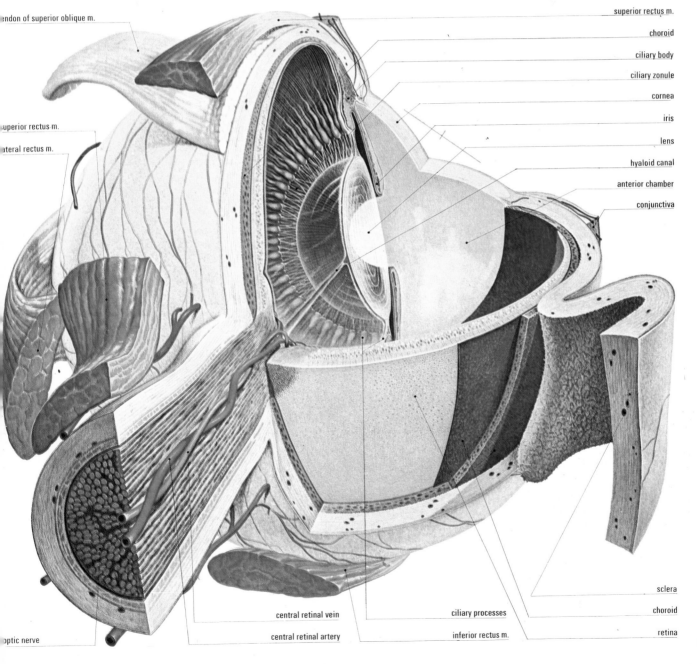

tendon of superior oblique m.

superior rectus m.

lateral rectus m.

optic nerve

central retinal vein

central retinal artery

ciliary processes

inferior rectus m.

superior rectus m.

choroid

ciliary body

ciliary zonule

cornea

iris

lens

hyaloid canal

anterior chamber

conjunctiva

sclera

choroid

retina

vision

Embedded securely in orbital fat (CAT scan, right) and acted on by the external ocular muscles (below), the eyeball consists of three main layers; the photosensitive retinal layer lining the pigmented choroid, and a tough outer fibrous layer, the sclera, which is continuous with the clear cornea. The anterior and posterior chambers in contact with the lens are occupied by aqueous humor. Interference with its drainage can cause a rise in intra-ocular pressure and glaucoma. The main globe of the eye contains the gel-like vitreous humor.

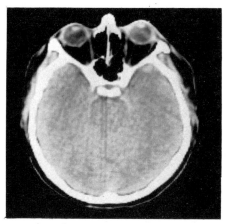

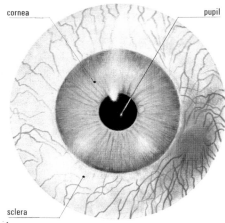

cornea

pupil

sclera

A marginal ulcer with marked conjunctival infection. Below, an ulcer invading the cornea surface. The cornea has a rich sensory innervation (below left) via the ciliary branch of the opthalmic (trigeminal) nerve.

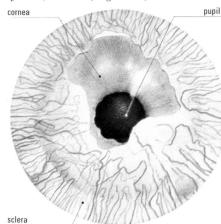

cornea

pupil

sclera

Two kinds of eyelid inflammation: a stye originates with suppuration in an eyelash sebaceous gland whereas a chalazion develops within the eyelid space, in a Meibomian or tarsal gland.

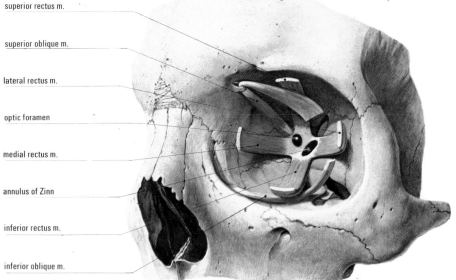

superior rectus m.

superior oblique m.

lateral rectus m.

optic foramen

medial rectus m.

annulus of Zinn

inferior rectus m.

inferior oblique m.

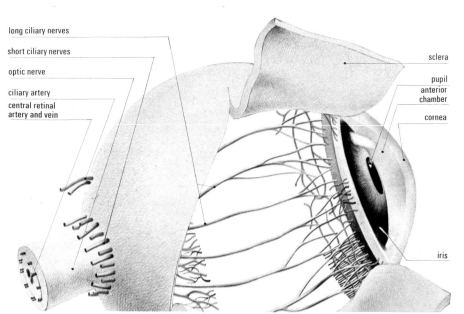

long ciliary nerves

short ciliary nerves

optic nerve

ciliary artery

central retinal artery and vein

sclera

pupil
anterior chamber

cornea

iris

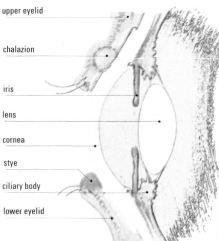

upper eyelid

chalazion

iris

lens

cornea

stye

ciliary body

lower eyelid

For efficient transmission of light the cornea must be kept clean and warm. These requirements are met by the constant secretion of tear fluid by the lacrimal glands; this is swept over the surface of the eye by blinking movements of the eyelids before collecting in the lacus lacrimalis. Here it drains into the nasolacrimal duct via the lacrimal canaliculi, and passes down to the nose. The eyelids are lined with a transparent mucous membrane, the conjunctiva, which is reflected forwards over the sclera to form the corneal epithelium anteriorly. The conjunctiva is easily inflamed, by bacteria (above right) and viruses (below right).

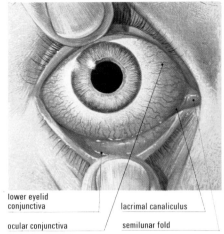

lower eyelid conjunctiva
ocular conjunctiva
lacrimal canaliculus
semilunar fold
upper eyelid conjunctiva

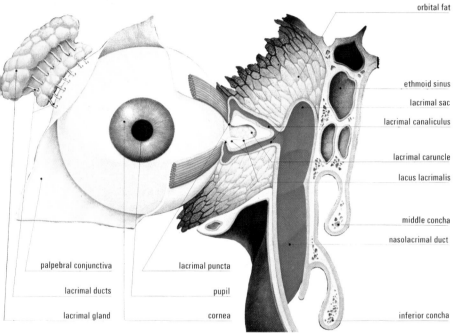

orbital fat
ethmoid sinus
lacrimal sac
lacrimal canaliculus
lacrimal caruncle
lacus lacrimalis
middle concha
nasolacrimal duct
inferior concha

palpebral conjunctiva
lacrimal ducts
lacrimal gland
lacrimal puncta
pupil
cornea

The cornea and lens may also be involved in pathological processes (right). In the upper row: punctate keratitis with spots disseminated over the corneal surface; dendritic keratitis with a starfish-like ulcer overlying the cornea, and disciform keratitis showing a flat circular opacity in the center of the cornea. The lower illustrations are of a cortical cataract with marked turbidity of the lens, a nuclear cataract and, finally, a cataract formed secondary to previous trauma.

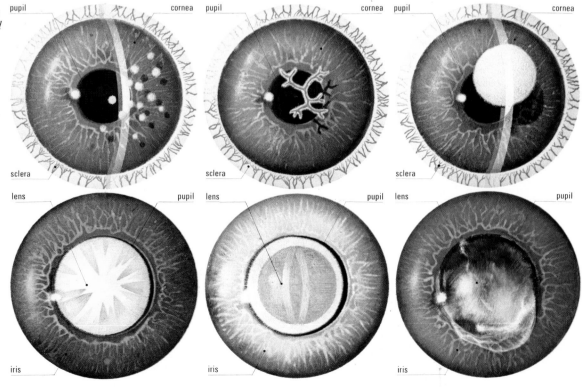

pupil   cornea   pupil   cornea   pupil   cornea
sclera   sclera   sclera
lens   pupil   lens   pupil   lens   pupil
iris   iris   iris

The retinal lining is a highly complex and vascular structure consisting of about ten separate layers, and includes the rod and cone photoreceptor cells (below) with their many ganglionic connections, blood vessels and supportive cells. At the macula, the optical 'center' of the eye (near right) the lining is much thinner and consists almost entirely of cones for very high quality visual interpretation. Seen through an opthalmoscope, the retinal fundus can be badly affected in diabetes mellitus (far right) with engorged vessels and many exudates. Beyond this are two different types of retinal detachment and (facing page, far right) their typical appearance after re-attachment using a laser beam.

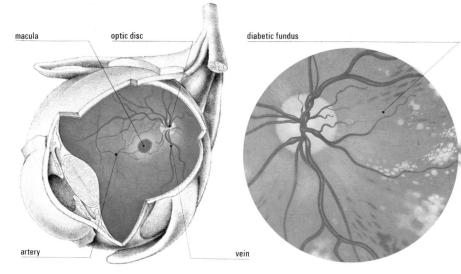

macula   optic disc   diabetic fundus

artery   vein

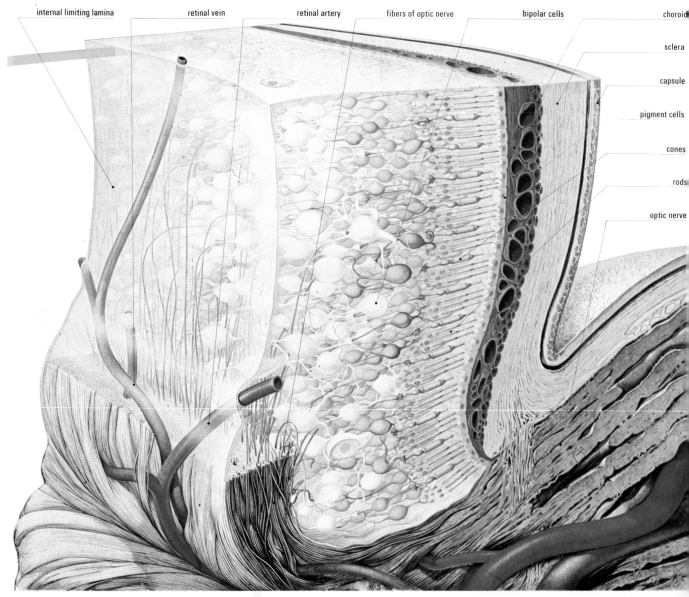

internal limiting lamina   retinal vein   retinal artery   fibers of optic nerve   bipolar cells   choroid

sclera

capsule

pigment cells

cones

rods

optic nerve

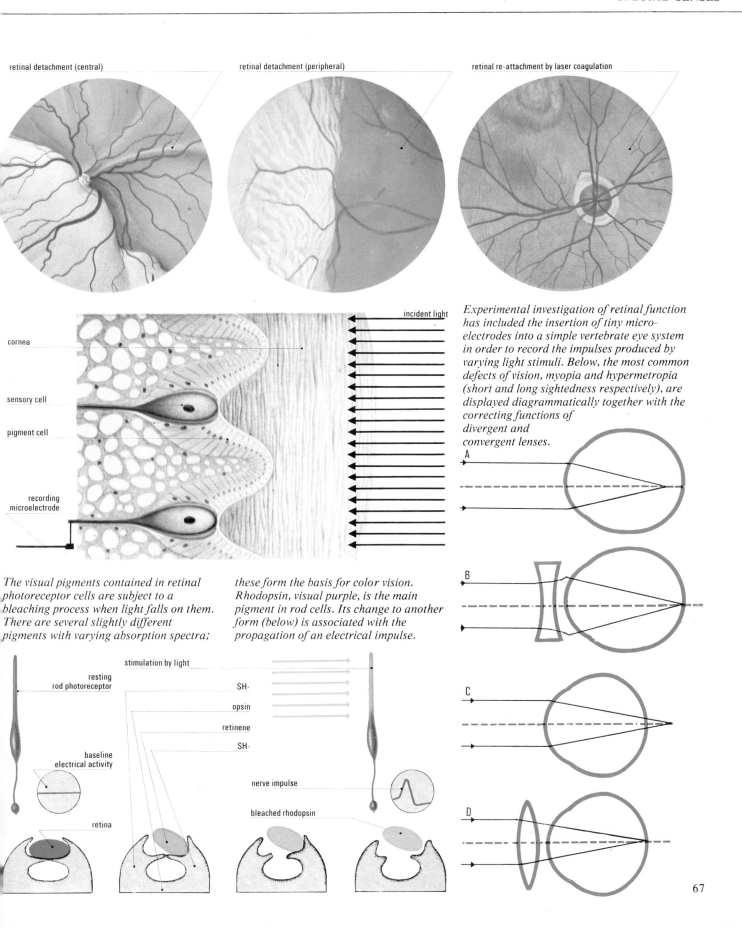

retinal detachment (central)

retinal detachment (peripheral)

retinal re-attachment by laser coagulation

incident light

cornea

sensory cell

pigment cell

recording microelectrode

Experimental investigation of retinal function has included the insertion of tiny micro-electrodes into a simple vertebrate eye system in order to record the impulses produced by varying light stimuli. Below, the most common defects of vision, myopia and hypermetropia (short and long sightedness respectively), are displayed diagrammatically together with the correcting functions of divergent and convergent lenses.

A

B

C

D

The visual pigments contained in retinal photoreceptor cells are subject to a bleaching process when light falls on them. There are several slightly different pigments with varying absorption spectra;

these form the basis for color vision. Rhodopsin, visual purple, is the main pigment in rod cells. Its change to another form (below) is associated with the propagation of an electrical impulse.

stimulation by light

resting rod photoreceptor

SH-

opsin

retinene

SH-

baseline electrical activity

nerve impulse

bleached rhodopsin

retina

smell

Man has a less well developed sense of smell than many animals, but olfaction has considerable importance in certain aspects of his social and sexual behaviour. The olfactory epithelium is located over the upper part of the nasal septum and superior concha (right). The receptor cell dendrites project into the epithelium as fine cilia covered with a thin layer of mucinous liquid.

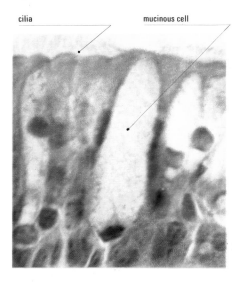

cilia   mucinous cell

The exact details of olfactory mechanisms are still uncertain, but it is postulated that for every major type of airborne molecule causing odor (below left) there are specific receptor sites (below right) that respond to them. The pattern of response also affects the brain's interpretation.

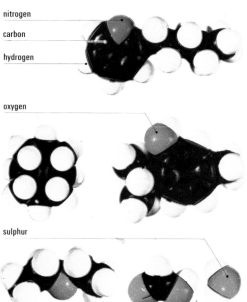

nitrogen

carbon

hydrogen

oxygen

sulphur

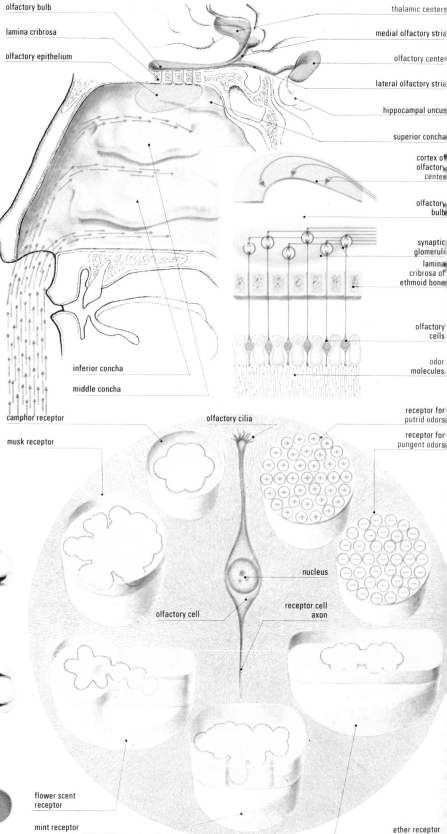

olfactory bulb

lamina cribrosa

olfactory epithelium

thalamic centers

medial olfactory stria

olfactory center

lateral olfactory stria

hippocampal uncus

superior concha

cortex of olfactory center

olfactory bulb

synaptic glomeruli

lamina cribrosa of ethmoid bone

olfactory cells

odor molecules

inferior concha

middle concha

camphor receptor

musk receptor

olfactory cilia

receptor for putrid odors

receptor for pungent odors

nucleus

olfactory cell

receptor cell axon

flower scent receptor

mint receptor

ether receptor

aste

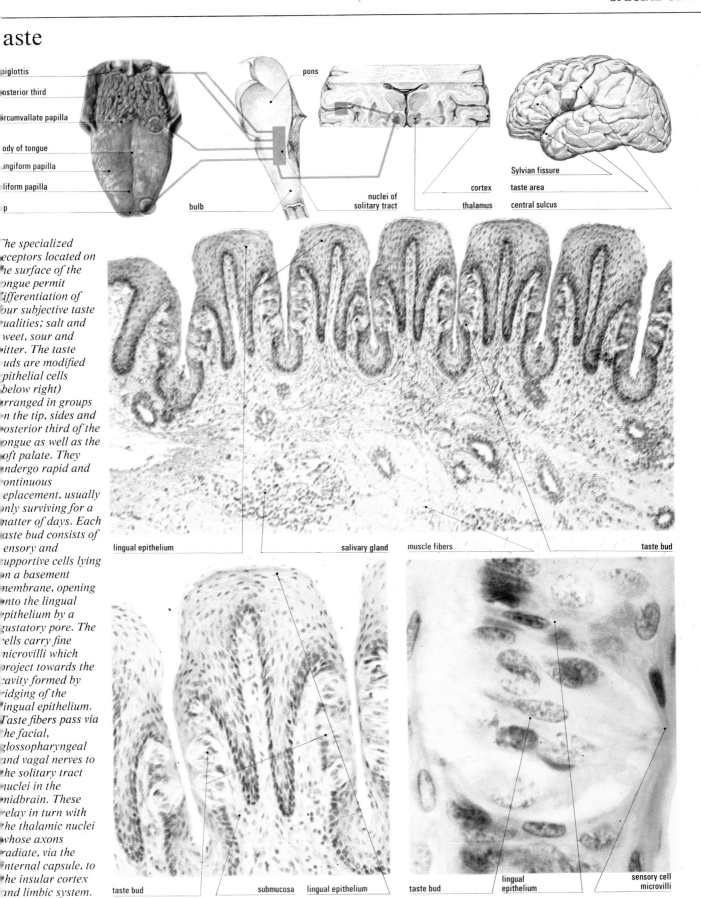

piglottis

osterior third

ircumvallate papilla

ody of tongue

ungiform papilla

liform papilla

p

bulb

pons

nuclei of
solitary tract

cortex

thalamus

Sylvian fissure

taste area

central sulcus

The specialized
receptors located on
the surface of the
tongue permit
differentiation of
four subjective taste
qualities; salt and
sweet, sour and
bitter. The taste
buds are modified
epithelial cells
(below right)
arranged in groups
on the tip, sides and
posterior third of the
tongue as well as the
soft palate. They
undergo rapid and
continuous
replacement, usually
only surviving for a
matter of days. Each
taste bud consists of
sensory and
supportive cells lying
on a basement
membrane, opening
onto the lingual
epithelium by a
gustatory pore. The
cells carry fine
microvilli which
project towards the
cavity formed by
ridging of the
lingual epithelium.
Taste fibers pass via
the facial,
glossopharyngeal
and vagal nerves to
the solitary tract
nuclei in the
midbrain. These
relay in turn with
the thalamic nuclei
whose axons
radiate, via the
internal capsule, to
the insular cortex
and limbic system.

lingual epithelium

salivary gland

muscle fibers

taste bud

taste bud

submucosa

lingual epithelium

taste bud

lingual
epithelium

sensory cell
microvilli

69

hearing

The human auditory range extends from 20 to 20,000 hz (cycles per second). Sound waves are formed by molecular vibrations of the air which vary in their intensity and frequency. These are collected by the external ear and transmitted to the tympanic membrane (below) which in turn sets in motion the auditory ossicles of the middle ear (below, right). These act as a bent lever to transfer the movements with increased force via the foramen ovale to the perilymph of the inner ear (lower left).

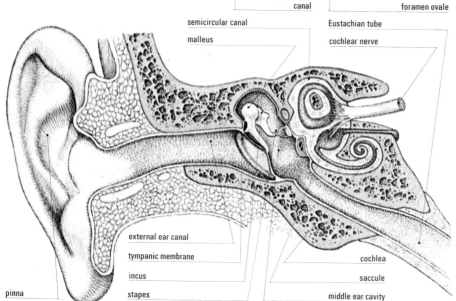

ampulla
anterior semicircular canal
vestibule
lateral semicircular canal
posterior semicircular canal
cochlea
foramen rotundum
foramen ovale

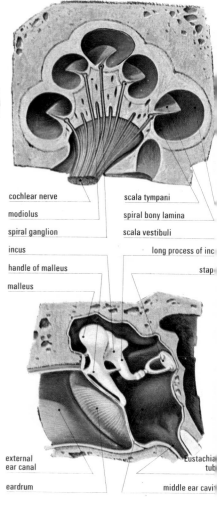

cochlear nerve
modiolus
spiral ganglion
incus
handle of malleus
malleus
scala tympani
spiral bony lamina
scala vestibuli
long process of inc
stap

semicircular canal
malleus
Eustachian tube
cochlear nerve

external ear canal
tympanic membrane
incus
pinna
stapes
cochlea
saccule
middle ear cavity

external ear canal
eardrum
Eustachia tub
middle ear cavi

The inner ear has bony and membranous labyrinthine components. Three semicircular and one cochlear duct lie

respectively in bony semicircular canals and a spirally arranged cochlear canal (above, middle and right). The cochlear

duct contains the organ of hearing, whereas the semicircular canals provide sensory input about balance and orientati

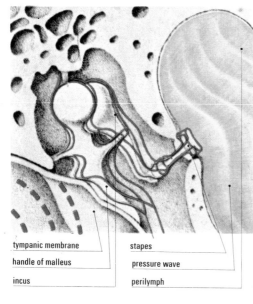

tympanic membrane
handle of malleus
incus
stapes
pressure wave
perilymph

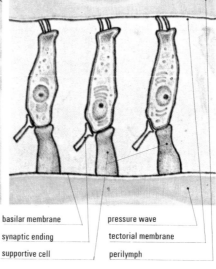

basilar membrane
synaptic ending
supportive cell
pressure wave
tectorial membrane
perilymph

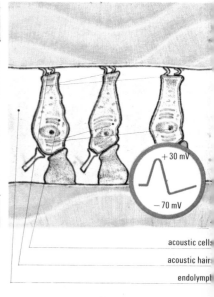

+30 mV
−70 mV

acoustic cells
acoustic hair
endolymph

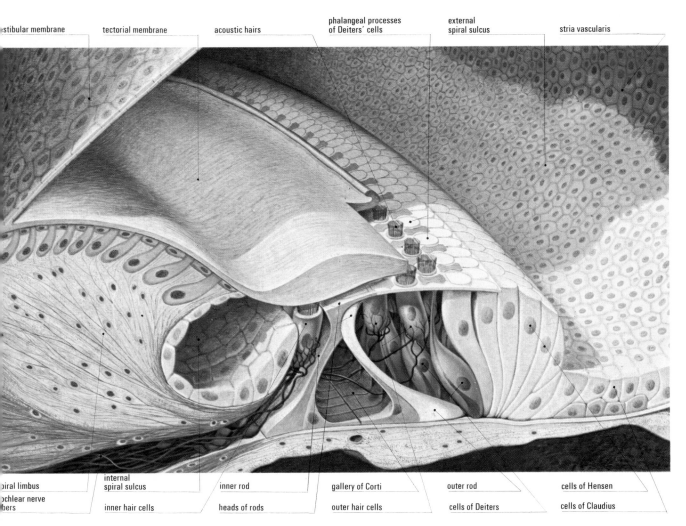

vestibular membrane | tectorial membrane | acoustic hairs | phalangeal processes of Deiters' cells | external spiral sulcus | stria vascularis

spiral limbus | internal spiral sulcus | inner rod | gallery of Corti | outer rod | cells of Hensen
cochlear nerve fibers | inner hair cells | heads of rods | outer hair cells | cells of Deiters | cells of Claudius

The cochlear canal is ridged internally by a bony crest which is attached, by the basilar membrane and spiral ligament, to the outer wall of the canal. The basilar membrane contains the spiral organ of Corti, two rows of specialized auditory cells. These lie on either side of a tunnel, together with specialized supporting cells (above), and their hair-like processes project through a reticular lamina to become embedded in the tectorial membrane. Vibrations of perilymph set up shearing stresses between the basilar and tectorial membranes (facing page, lower right). Compression of the hair cells results in the generation of cochlear nerve impulses. The ampulla (right) of a semicircular duct contains a crest of specialized hair cells, sensitive to the internal endolymph currents that result from changes in head position or acceleration and deceleration of the body.

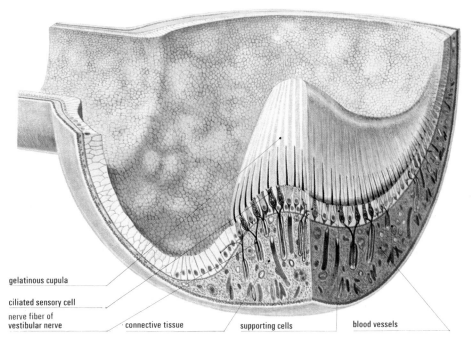

gelatinous cupula

ciliated sensory cell

nerve fiber of vestibular nerve | connective tissue | supporting cells | blood vessels

71

touch

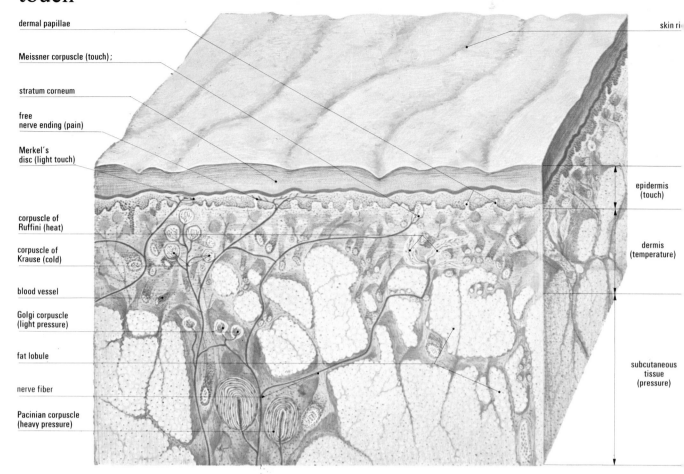

dermal papillae

skin ri

Meissner corpuscle (touch);

stratum corneum

free
nerve ending (pain)

Merkel's
disc (light touch)

epidermis
(touch)

corpuscle of
Ruffini (heat)

corpuscle of
Krause (cold)

dermis
(temperature)

blood vessel

Golgi corpuscle
(light pressure)

fat lobule

subcutaneous
tissue
(pressure)

nerve fiber

Pacinian corpuscle
(heavy pressure)

*The skin forms a protective barrier
between the body and its external
environment, and is richly equipped
with sensors to monitor changes in
exterior physical conditions. The
actual receptor cells show a wide
variation in structure and location,
some lying superficially and sensitive
to heat or light touch, others more
deeply placed and activated only by
heavy pressure. The simplest forms of
sensor are the myelinated and non-
myelinated 'free endings' widely
distributed throughout the dermis and
lowest layers of the epidermis. In hairy
skin these often lie in close association
with hair follicles, and here too the
nerve endings are frequently modified
into Merkel's discs. The density of
sensor distribution varies. Two-point
discrimination (vital to blind Braille
readers) is at its highest level in the
finger tips due to a large concentration
of Meissner corpuscles there. On the
right is a histological section of a
lamellated Pacinian corpuscle,
generally found in the deeper layers of
the skin.*

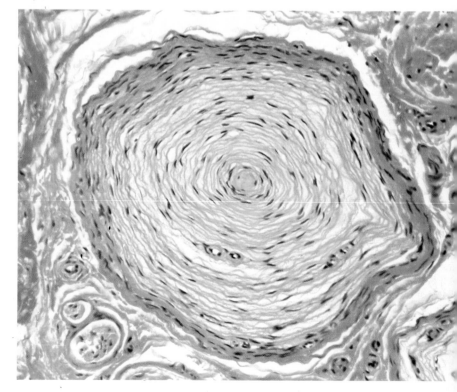

he respiratory apparatus

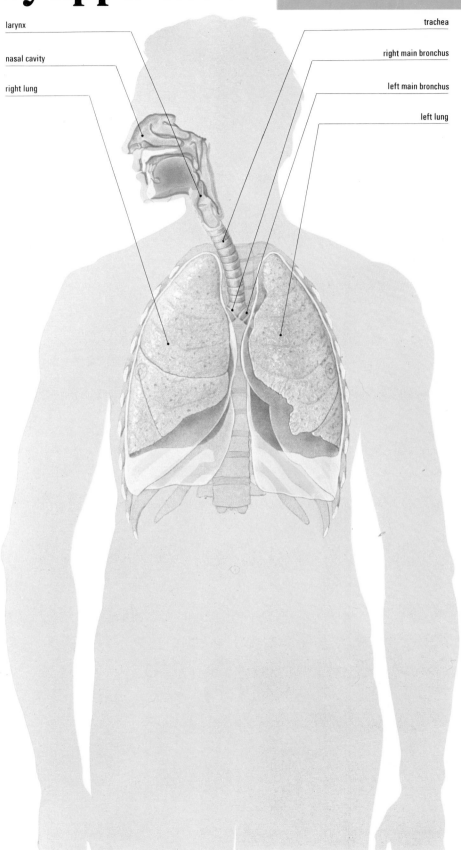

xygen is, literally, vital to life. The same
tracellular metabolic processes that use
ygen to sustain them also produce car-
n dioxide. In simple single-celled crea-
res these gases merely diffuse in and out
cording to pressure gradients; much
rger creatures like man have had to
velop a blood transport system for their
rriage to and from the tissues. Gaseous
change takes place in paired specialized
ructures, the lungs, which are connected
the outside air by a breathing tube, the
spiratory tract. The upper respiratory
act runs from the nose to the larynx. The
ing mucous membrane is ciliated and
s a rich blood supply; inspired air is
armed to body temperature and satur-
ed with water vapour. Inhaled foreign
rticles are trapped in a sticky mucus
yer and wafted by ciliary action to-
ards the pharynx for expulsion by
ughing. The same cough reflex aids the
rynx in its second line protective capa-
ty, against bigger particles; it also closes
f during the act of swallowing to pre-
nt food or liquid entering the lungs. But
e unique function of the larynx is phona-
on, the formation of speech sounds.
oupled with precise neural control of
latal and labial muscles, the facility of
eech has been an essential feature in
an's evolutionary dominance. Below the
rynx lies a membranous tube, the
achea (windpipe), buttressed by carti-
ginous rings. Some 11 cm long in the
ult, it descends through the superior
ediastinum of the thorax before dividing
to main bronchi for each lung root.
ese divide in turn into lobar and seg-
ental bronchi, then progressively smaller
onchioles which terminate in the
veolar sacs. The alveoli are thin-walled
ouches, shaped like bunches of grapes.
though compressed into a small volume
e thoracic cavity) there are 300 million
them to provide a surface area for gas
change that is thirty times greater than
e body's surface area – some 70 square
eters for an adult male. Richly investing
e alveolar sacs, the endothelium of the
lmonary capillary network adds very
tle thickness to the barrier between
ood and alveolar air. The oxygen/car-
n dioxide exchange is rapid since the red
lls spend under a second actually in the
lmonary capillaries before returning to
e left side of the heart for systemic distri-
ition. The mechanical work required to
ntilate the lungs is performed by the
spiratory muscles. Elastic recoil against
spiration gives passive help to expira-
on, but there is a constant component of
rways resistance to overcome – a factor
major importance when the airways are
rrowed by disease.

larynx

nasal cavity

right lung

trachea

right main bronchus

left main bronchus

left lung

The structural relationship between the upper respiratory tract and the pharynx is a complex one; a posterior view (right) shows the pharyngeal walls reflected from the midline. Below, a sagittal section through the skull with the nasopharynx and pharynx highlighted in color. The arterial anastomosis between the greater palatine, sphenopalatine, and labial branch of the facial artery is a common site for nosebleeds (epistaxes). The pituitary gland is separated from the nasopharynx only by the sphenoidal sinus; this is a possible approach for pituitary surgery. More posteriorly is the pharyngeal opening of the auditory (Eustachian) tube by which middle ear cavity pressure is equalized with that of the exterior. The thermograph (below) shows the face of a patient with a tumor of the right maxillary sinus, a hollow cavity lined with modified respiratory epithelium and lying beneath the orbit.

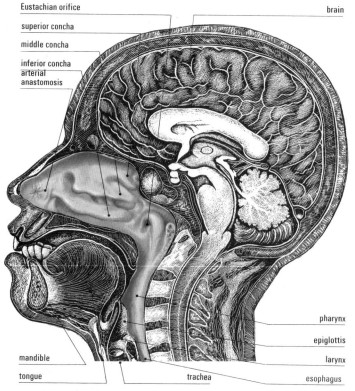

Eustachian orifice
superior concha
middle concha
inferior concha
arterial anastomosis
brain
mandible
tongue
trachea
pharynx
epiglottis
larynx
esophagus

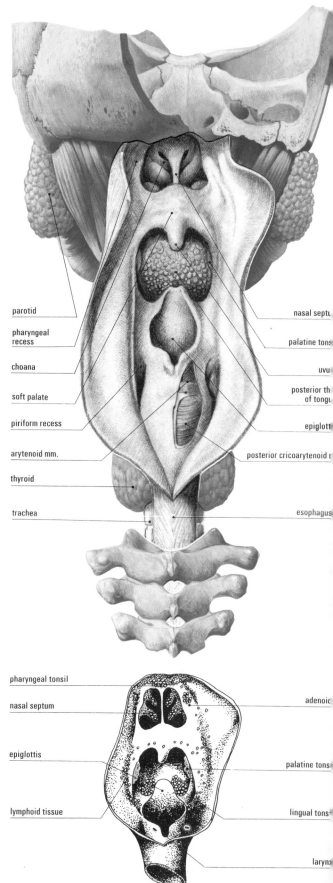

parotid
pharyngeal recess
choana
soft palate
piriform recess
arytenoid mm.
thyroid
trachea
nasal septu
palatine tons
uvu
posterior th of tongu
epiglott
posterior cricoarytenoid n
esophagus

pharyngeal tonsil
nasal septum
epiglottis
lymphoid tissue
adenoic
palatine tons
lingual tons
larynx

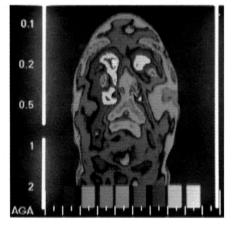

The lymphatic ring (of Waldeyer, right) surrounds the entrance to the pharynx. Small collections of lymphoid tissue lie between the larger aggregations of the palatine, lingual and pharyngeal tonsils. Chronic infection in this area may require surgical treatment by removal.

The larynx is anterior to the pharynx. As well as being part of the respiratory tract, it is the organ of phonation. It also has a sphincteric function to raise airway pressure during sneezing and coughing. With a cartilaginous and ligamentous framework, it is acted on by numerous intrinsic and extrinsic muscles (below and left). The inner aspect of each wall is modified into two transverse ridges, the false and true vocal cords, which form a thin ditch aligned across the axis of air flow. During phonation, the lower pair of vocal cords are set into a vibrating motion by expiring air. The sound produced has a frequency dependent on the degree of cord tension; this is varied by muscles acting on the arytenoid cartilages. As voice pitch rises, the length of the vocal cords may increase by half. Motor innervation of the larynx is mainly via the recurrent laryngeal branch of the vagus nerve, a structure easily damaged during thyroid surgery.

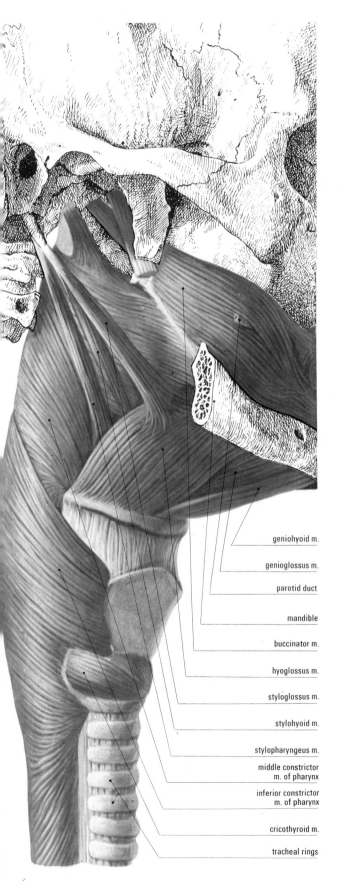

geniohyoid m.

genioglossus m.

parotid duct

mandible

buccinator m.

hyoglossus m.

styloglossus m.

stylohyoid m.

stylopharyngeus m.

middle constrictor m. of pharynx

inferior constrictor m. of pharynx

cricothyroid m.

tracheal rings

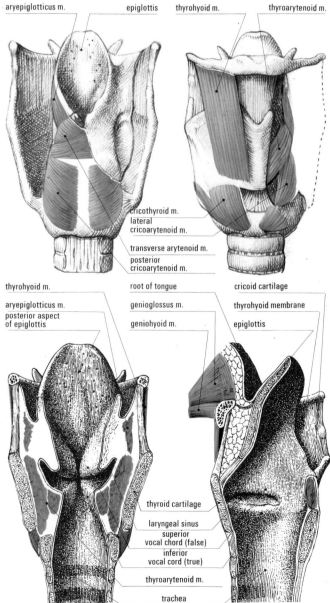

aryepiglotticus m.

epiglottis

thyrohyoid m.

thyroarytenoid m.

cricothyroid m.
lateral cricoarytenoid m.

transverse arytenoid m.

posterior cricoarytenoid m.

thyrohyoid m.

root of tongue

cricoid cartilage

aryepiglotticus m.
posterior aspect of epiglottis

genioglossus m.

thyrohyoid membrane

geniohyoid m.

epiglottis

thyroid cartilage

laryngeal sinus

superior vocal chord (false)

inferior vocal cord (true)

thyroarytenoid m.

trachea

A sagittal section (below) through the larynx and upper trachea is displayed along with anterior and posterior views of the cartilage framework of the area. The reinforcing rings of the trachea are incomplete posteriorly, giving a flattened aspect where it lies against the esophagus in the thorax. The upper borders of the thyroid cartilage fuse in the midline to form an easily palpable subcutaneous laryngeal prominence, the 'Adam's apple'. The epiglottis consists of elastic fibrocartilage, whereas the thyroid, cricoid and tracheal cartilages have a hyaline structure (right) which may undergo calcification in later life.

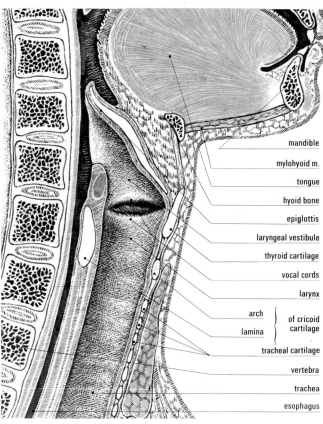

mandible

mylohyoid m.

tongue

hyoid bone

epiglottis

laryngeal vestibule

thyroid cartilage

vocal cords

larynx

arch

lamina

of cricoid cartilage

tracheal cartilage

vertebra

trachea

esophagus

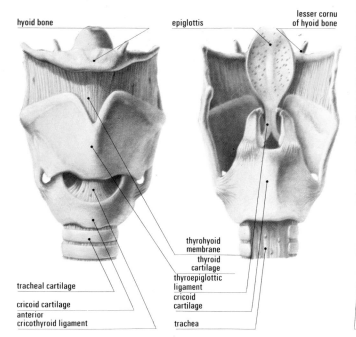

hyoid bone

epiglottis

lesser cornu of hyoid bone

thyrohyoid membrane

thyroid cartilage

thyroepiglottic ligament

cricoid cartilage

trachea

tracheal cartilage

cricoid cartilage

anterior cricothyroid ligament

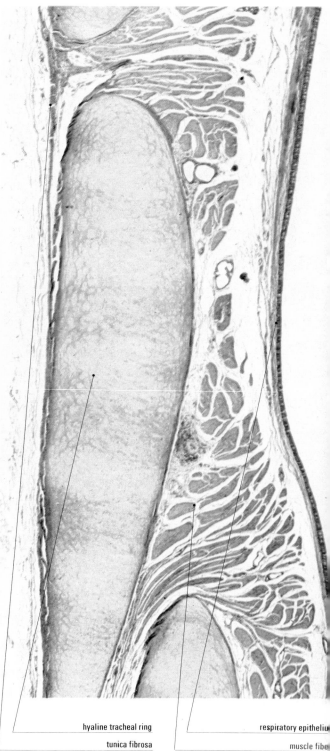

hyaline tracheal ring

tunica fibrosa

respiratory epithelium

muscle fibre

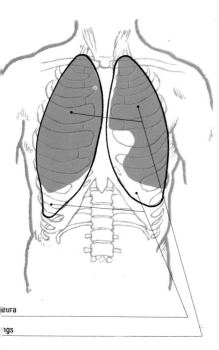

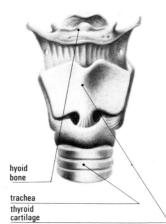

hyoid
bone

trachea
thyroid
cartilage

eura

ngs

The surface marking of the lungs and pleura (left) shows an indentation of the left upper lobe caused by the heart – the cardiac notch. There are two pleural layers; parietal and visceral. The visceral pleura closely invests each lung, the parietal pleura lines the chest wall, mediastinum and diaphragm. The blood vessels of the lung are well demonstrated in the CAT scan (below right) taken just below the tracheal bifurcation.

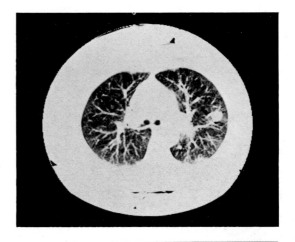

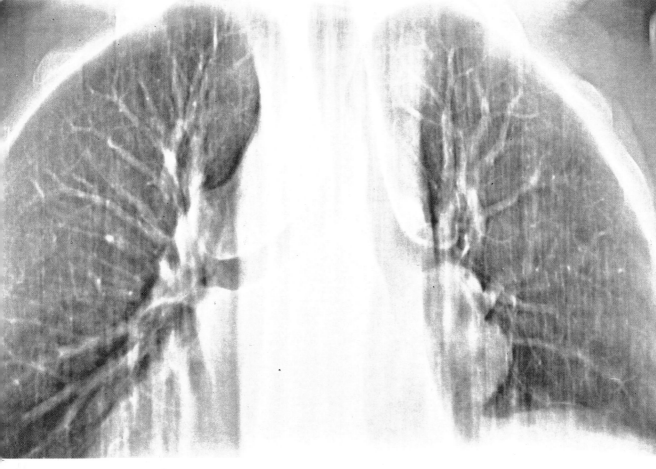

A xerotomographic X-ray of the mediastinum (above), taken from behind looking forwards, has blurred out all structures except the trachea and main bronchi. On the right there is marked bronchial narrowing due to a squamous cell carcinoma.

77

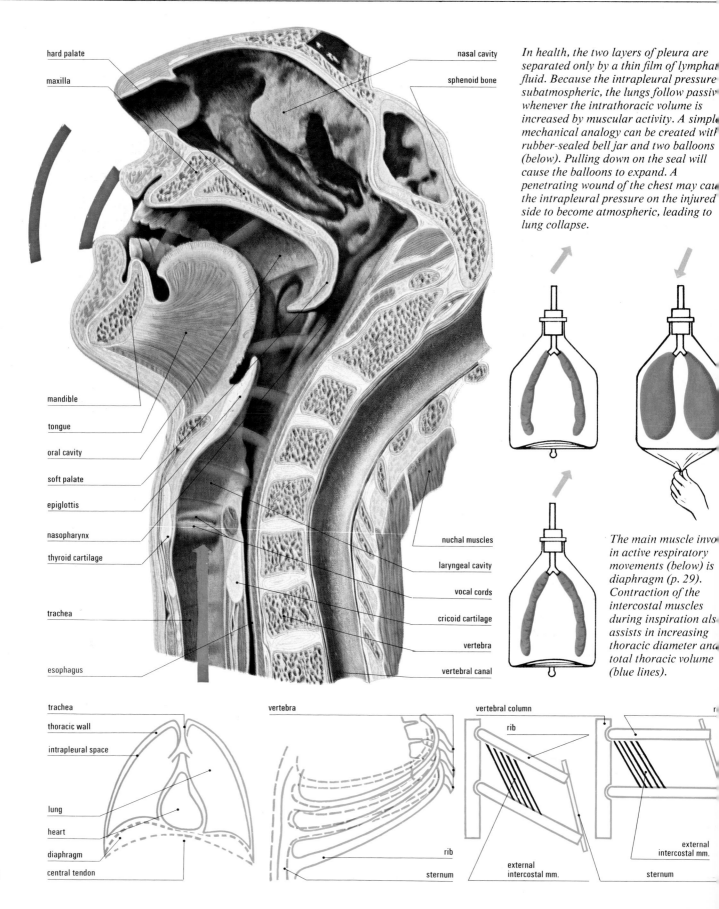

hard palate

maxilla

nasal cavity

sphenoid bone

mandible

tongue

oral cavity

soft palate

epiglottis

nasopharynx

thyroid cartilage

trachea

esophagus

nuchal muscles

laryngeal cavity

vocal cords

cricoid cartilage

vertebra

vertebral canal

In health, the two layers of pleura are separated only by a thin film of lymphatic fluid. Because the intrapleural pressure is subatmospheric, the lungs follow passively whenever the intrathoracic volume is increased by muscular activity. A simple mechanical analogy can be created with a rubber-sealed bell jar and two balloons (below). Pulling down on the seal will cause the balloons to expand. A penetrating wound of the chest may cause the intrapleural pressure on the injured side to become atmospheric, leading to lung collapse.

The main muscle involved in active respiratory movements (below) is the diaphragm (p. 29). Contraction of the intercostal muscles during inspiration also assists in increasing thoracic diameter and total thoracic volume (blue lines).

trachea

thoracic wall

intrapleural space

lung

heart

diaphragm

central tendon

vertebra

rib

sternum

vertebral column

rib

external intercostal mm.

external intercostal mm.

sternum

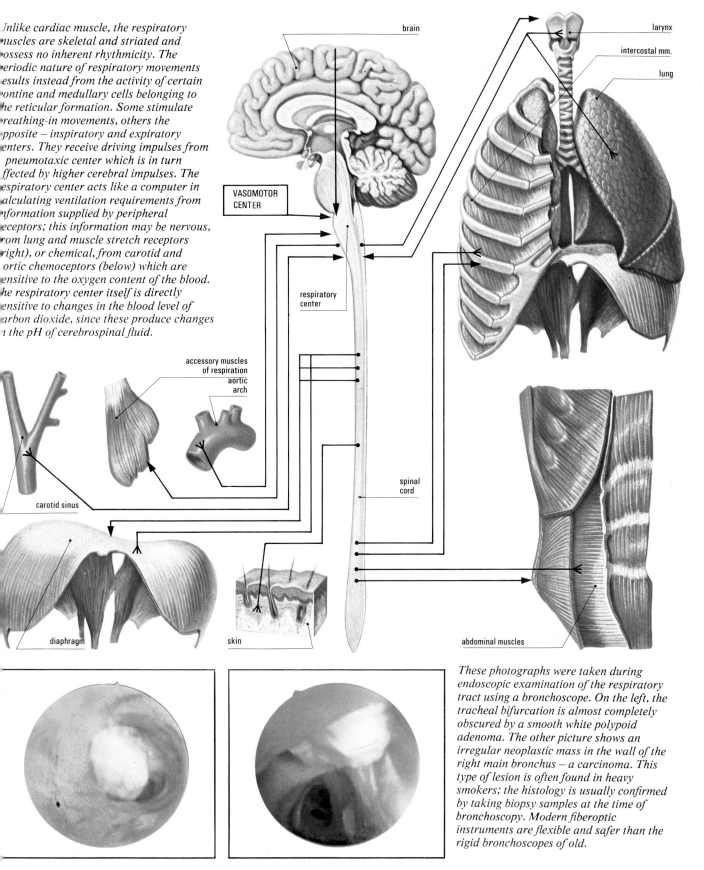

Unlike cardiac muscle, the respiratory muscles are skeletal and striated and possess no inherent rhythmicity. The periodic nature of respiratory movements results instead from the activity of certain pontine and medullary cells belonging to the reticular formation. Some stimulate breathing-in movements, others the opposite – inspiratory and expiratory centers. They receive driving impulses from a pneumotaxic center which is in turn affected by higher cerebral impulses. The respiratory center acts like a computer in calculating ventilation requirements from information supplied by peripheral receptors; this information may be nervous, from lung and muscle stretch receptors (right), or chemical, from carotid and aortic chemoceptors (below) which are sensitive to the oxygen content of the blood. The respiratory center itself is directly sensitive to changes in the blood level of carbon dioxide, since these produce changes in the pH of cerebrospinal fluid.

brain

larynx

intercostal mm.

lung

VASOMOTOR CENTER

respiratory center

spinal cord

accessory muscles of respiration

aortic arch

carotid sinus

diaphragm

skin

abdominal muscles

These photographs were taken during endoscopic examination of the respiratory tract using a bronchoscope. On the left, the tracheal bifurcation is almost completely obscured by a smooth white polypoid adenoma. The other picture shows an irregular neoplastic mass in the wall of the right main bronchus – a carcinoma. This type of lesion is often found in heavy smokers; the histology is usually confirmed by taking biopsy samples at the time of bronchoscopy. Modern fiberoptic instruments are flexible and safer than the rigid bronchoscopes of old.

79

The palatine tonsils lie between the palatoglossal and palatopharyngeal folds at the back of the oropharynx (illustration upper left). As part of a lymphoid defensive ring they are frequently the sites of suppurative infection (middle right) along with the adenoids (upper right, viewed with a mirror) located in the posterior nasopharynx. Blockage of the nasopharynx and Eustachian tubes in childhood, as a result of chronic infection, can affect the development of the skull. This in turn may give rise to the typical picture of a permanently mouth-breathing, slightly deaf adolescent with a pinched face, the 'adenoidal facies'. Surgical treatment of these problems involves their removal by tonsillectomy and adenoidectomy, both frequently performed operations. A cutting-edged adenotome and basket (middle left) is placed against the posterior nasopharynx and the adenoidal excrescences gently scraped away. In tonsillectomy, a guillotine is used to lever the tonsils away from the palatine pillars (below left) before they are cut free (below right) and then removed.

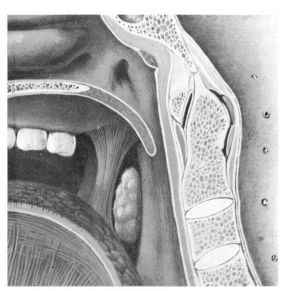

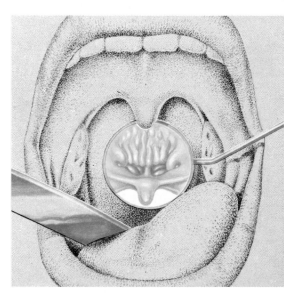

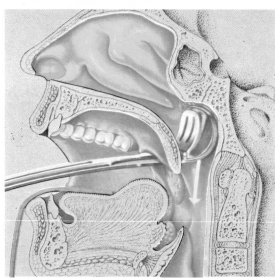

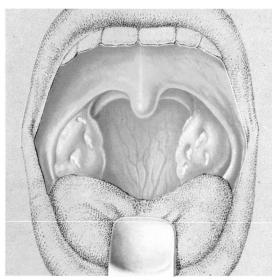

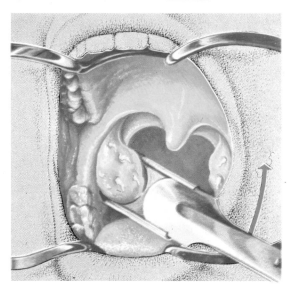

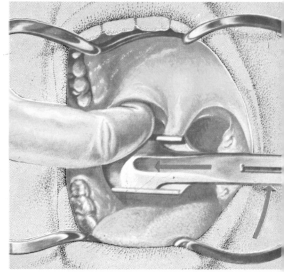

The digestive system

The digestive system consists of the alimentary canal and certain associated organs which are involved in the chewing, swallowing, breakdown and absorption of food as well as the expulsion from the body of what is left after these processes are complete. In the mouth, food is bathed in amylase-rich secretions of the salivary glands while mastication, involving teeth and tongue, breaks it up. With starch digestion already under way, the food (now converted into an alimentary bolus) is transferred to the next part of the alimentary tract by the reflex act of swallowing. The bolus traverses the esophagus in about ten seconds, and passes into the stomach which has a reservoir function and can hold some 1500 ml in the adult. Here it is minutely divided by churning peristaltic contraction waves and also mixed with gastric juice to form a paste called chyme. Gastric juice is rich in hydrochloric acid and the protein-splitting enzyme pepsin. The rate of gastric emptying depends on the degree of distension and the type of food ingested; marked delay occurs after a fatty meal due to release of a hormone by the small intestine. A muscular valve, the pylorus, controls the emptying process by opening after every four to five peristaltic waves. In the duodenum the chyme is exposed to the pancreatic juice which contains further carbohydrate, protein and fat splitting enzymes, the latter's effect helped considerably by the admixture of bile secreted by the liver. During transit through the small intestine the products of these digestive processes are absorbed both actively and passively, and transported directly to the liver in the portal venous system. The liver is the largest gland in the body and occupies the right hypochondrium. Of lobular structure, it receives some 1.5 liters of blood a minute. The liver cells have vital functions in storage and recombination of digestion products, the inactivation of hormones, the detoxification of drugs and poisons, and the formation and excretion of bile. The 1.5 meters of large intestine, running from the ileocecal valve to the anal margin, completes the 9 meters of alimentary tract. Its functions are related mainly to the absorption of water and electrolyte ions. The unabsorbable residue is concentrated in the descending colon as a fecal stool which is discharged periodically through the anal canal by the voluntary act of defecation. Despite wide differences in function, each section of the alimentary canal has the same basic structure: an epithelium, with secretory cells or glands; a subepithelial connective tissue layer, the lamina propria, with associated smooth muscle fibers, the muscularis mucosae; a nerve and blood vessel rich submucosa; two external muscle layers arranged in inner circular and outer longitudinal coats, and a covering serosa.

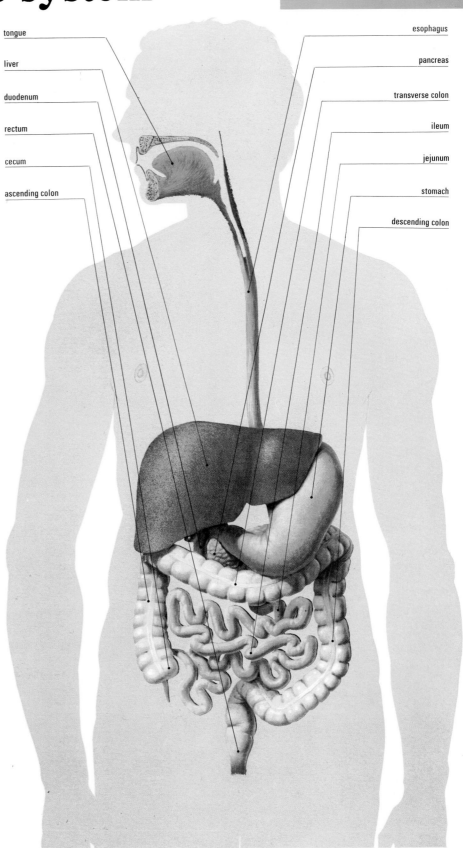

tongue

liver

duodenum

rectum

cecum

ascending colon

esophagus

pancreas

transverse colon

ileum

jejunum

stomach

descending colon

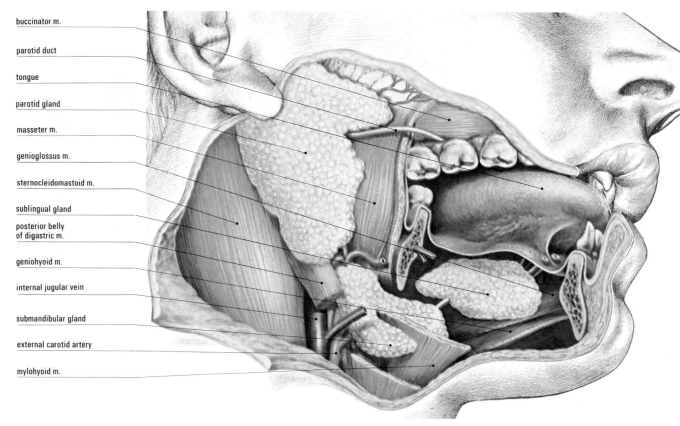

buccinator m.

parotid duct

tongue

parotid gland

masseter m.

genioglossus m.

sternocleidomastoid m.

sublingual gland

posterior belly
of digastric m.

geniohyoid m.

internal jugular vein

submandibular gland

external carotid artery

mylohyoid m.

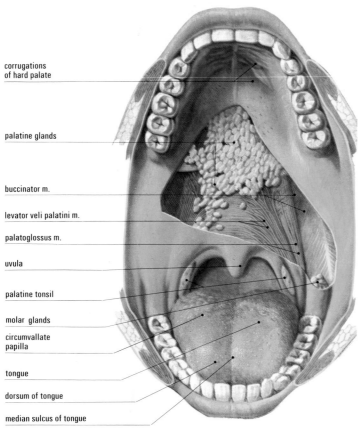

corrugations
of hard palate

palatine glands

buccinator m.

levator veli palatini m.

palatoglossus m.

uvula

palatine tonsil

molar glands

circumvallate
papilla

tongue

dorsum of tongue

median sulcus of tongue

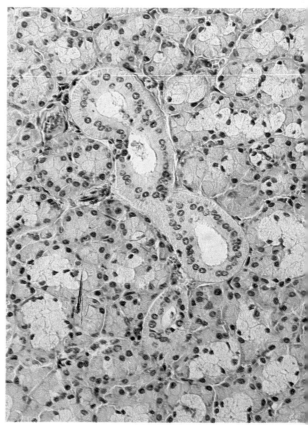

The three main paired salivary glands, parotid, sublingual and submandibular, are shown in greater detail on these pages together with their relationships to other superficial and deep tissues. Their structure is lobulated, with each lobule drained by a single branched ductule. These converge to form a salivary duct which drains into the oral cavity via a buccal opening. The secretory alveoli are generally a mixture of mucinous and serous, although the parotid gland contains only serous cells. A microphotograph (facing page, lower right) shows the predominantly mucinous nature of sublingual gland alveoli. The teeth are also accessory digestive organs. The dentition of mammals has several evolutionary advantages, including a set of deciduous or 'milk' teeth in growing jaws which are replaced by permanent teeth at a later age. Also, a harder and thicker tooth covering made of spatially oriented enamel prisms (highlighted, below right, by the polarizing microscope) gives better mechanical properties of wear and tear; this feature is also helped by the slightly flexible tooth mounting in periodontal ligament (below).

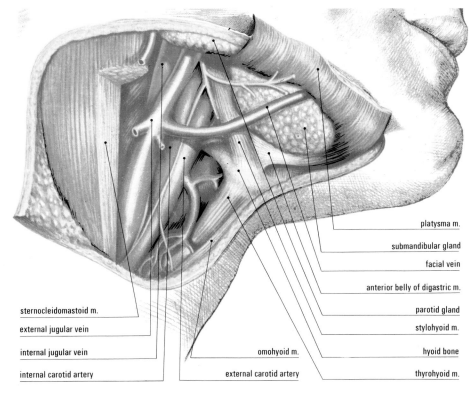

sternocleidomastoid m.

external jugular vein

internal jugular vein

internal carotid artery

omohyoid m.

external carotid artery

platysma m.

submandibular gland

facial vein

anterior belly of digastric m.

parotid gland

stylohyoid m.

hyoid bone

thyrohyoid m.

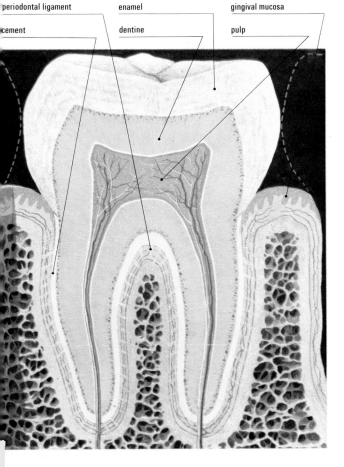

periodontal ligament

cement

enamel

dentine

gingival mucosa

pulp

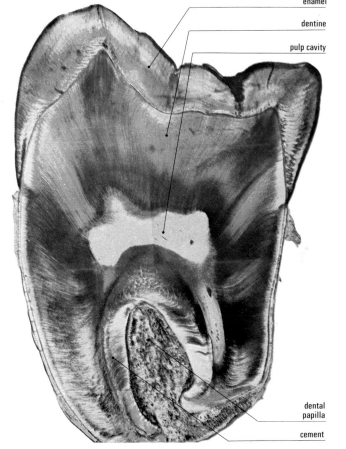

enamel

dentine

pulp cavity

dental papilla

cement

83

The esophagus is a muscular tube some 26 cm long which is continuous with the pharynx and connects it to the cardia of the stomach. Beginning at the level of the cricoid cartilage, opposite the sixth cervical vertebra, the esophagus lies anteriorly to the vertebral column as it passes through the thoracic mediastinum, where it has close relationships with the arch of the aorta and trachea (diagram left). After turning forwards at the level of the tenth thoracic vertebra, it pierces the diaphragm. The mechanical movements of deglutition, or swallowing, are discussed in more detail on pp. 92–93. The lining epithelium of the esophagus is of a non-keratinizing stratified squamous type. At the gastro-esophageal junction of the cardia (microphotograph, upper right) this changes suddenly into a simple columnar epithelium and a more glandular structure. Macroscopically, the lining mucous membrane of the stomach is thrown into numerous longitudinal folds which present a honeycomb appearance. Microscopically, the honeycombing is caused by a series of gastric pits (microphotograph, lower right). At the base of these structures are the openings of the gastric glands, which contain different cell types depending on the region of stomach being examined. Chief cells produce the protein splitting enzyme pepsin; oxyntic (or parietal) cells secrete hydrochloric acid, while columnar cells produce mucus which has both lubricant and protective effects.

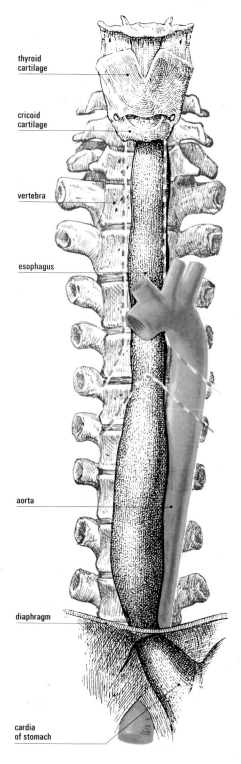

thyroid
cartilage

cricoid
cartilage

vertebra

esophagus

aorta

diaphragm

cardia
of stomach

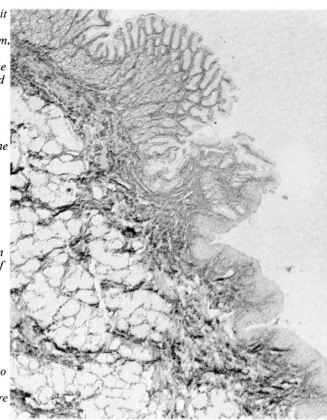

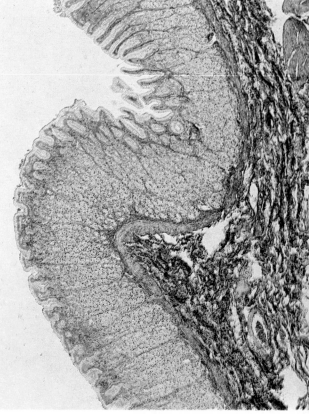

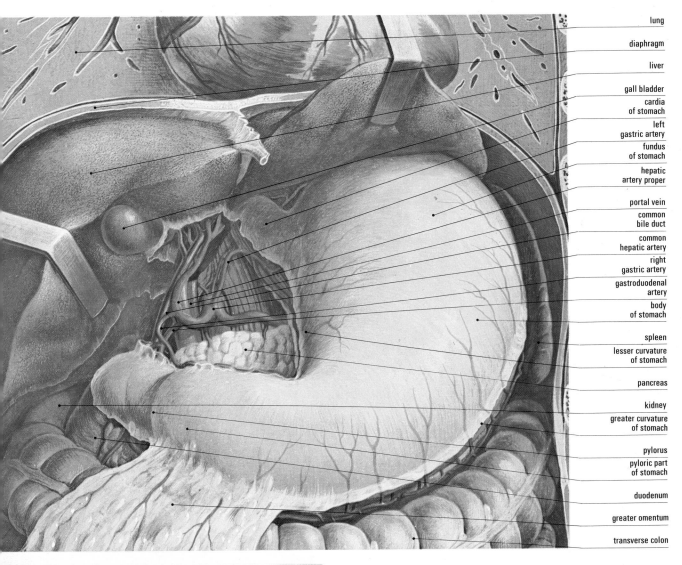

lung

diaphragm

liver

gall bladder

cardia
of stomach

left
gastric artery

fundus
of stomach

hepatic
artery proper

portal vein

common
bile duct

common
hepatic artery

right
gastric artery

gastroduodenal
artery

body
of stomach

spleen

lesser curvature
of stomach

pancreas

kidney

greater curvature
of stomach

pylorus

pyloric part
of stomach

duodenum

greater omentum

transverse colon

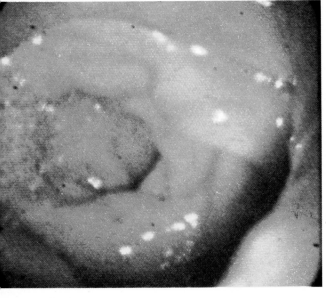

The stomach is the most dilated part of the digestive tract and lies in the upper left part of the abdomen. It has two curvatures, lesser and greater; two surfaces, anterior and posterior, and two orifices, cardiac and pyloric. The functions of the stomach are to act as a reservoir for food; to prepare it for entry into the intestines by warming, mixing and initiating digestion, and to pass it into the duodenum in appropriate amounts. The reservoir function is performed mainly by relaxation of muscular fibers in the body and fundus, whereas mixing occurs mainly in the pre-pyloric antrum. At the distal end of the stomach, the pyloric sphincter is a thickened part of the stomach's inner circular muscle layer. Occasionally it is hypertrophied in the neonate and requires splitting (pyloromyotomy) in order to relieve obstruction and vomiting. The glands of the pyloric antrum (seen left through an endoscope) are mainly mucous in type and also elaborate gastrin, a powerful hormone produced in response to food which increases stomach motility as well as stimulating the activity of chief and oxyntic cells.

85

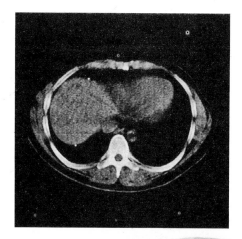

The liver weighs between 1.2 and 1.8 kg in the adult, lies beneath the right hemidiaphragm in the upper abdomen (CAT scan, left) and has two lobes, the left much smaller than the right. Although firm to the touch, liver tissue is extremely friable; because of the organ's great vascularity, wounds of the liver tend to be markedly hemorrhagic. The major external features of the liver are shown from anterior and inferior aspects (below). In microscopic terms the liver consists of columns of cells arranged radially in lobules around a centrilobular vein (below right). Between these columns lie two networks; blood sinusoids lined by vascular endothelium and Kupffer cells, and a large number of intralobular bile canaliculi. At the periphery of each lobule are several portal tracts containing branches of the hepatic artery, portal vein and intrahepatic bile ducts, together with fibrous connective tissue and small lymphatics. The blood supply to the liver is a mixed venous and arterial one. Although only a fifth of the supply is derived from the hepatic artery, this source provides half its oxygen requirements. The liver is thus vulnerable to damage in chronic hypoxia, or when metabolic (and oxygen) demands are high, as in thyrotoxicosis. A diffuse fibrosis affecting the whole liver and combined with nodular regeneration of lobule cells is termed cirrhosis. The commonest type of this condition is portal cirrhosis associated with poor nutrition and/or a high alcohol intake. The disturbances of liver architecture cause obstruction of the portal venous radicles, leading to portal hypertension and splenomegaly. This feature is well shown by the scintigram (facing page, lower) which is displayed beneath anterior and oblique views of normal liver parenchyma.

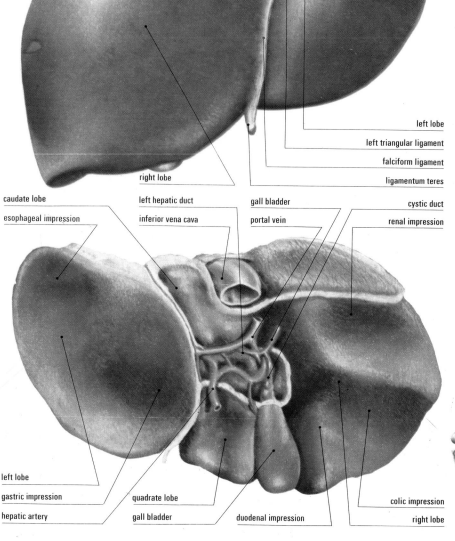

left lobe
left triangular ligament
falciform ligament
ligamentum teres
right lobe
caudate lobe
esophageal impression
left hepatic duct
inferior vena cava
gall bladder
portal vein
cystic duct
renal impression
left lobe
gastric impression
hepatic artery
quadrate lobe
gall bladder
duodenal impression
colic impression
right lobe

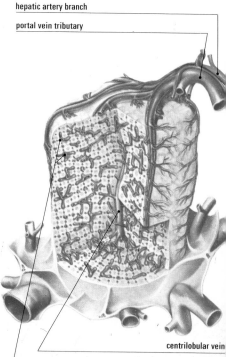

bile ductule
hepatic artery branch
portal vein tributary
centrilobular vein
sinusoids

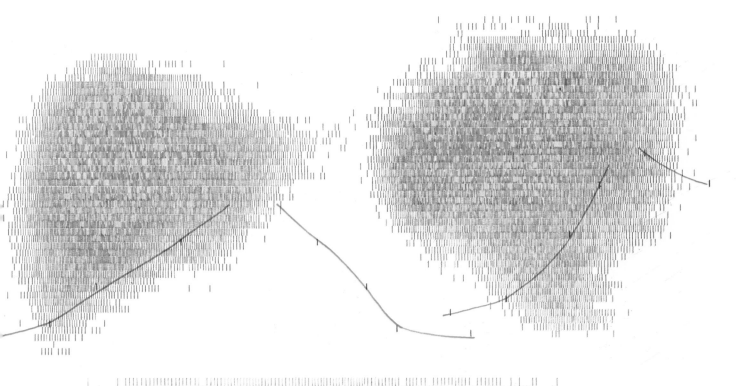

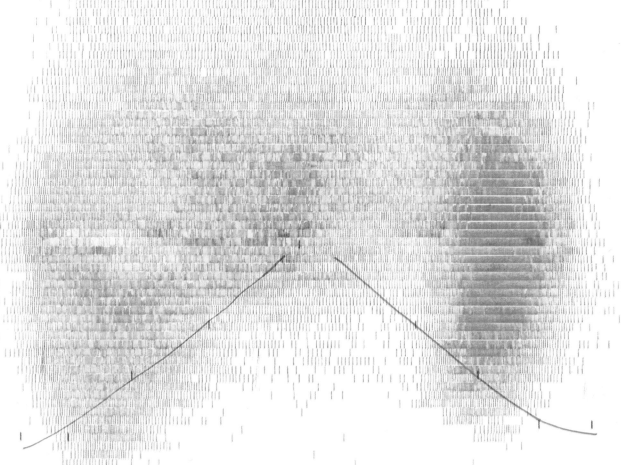

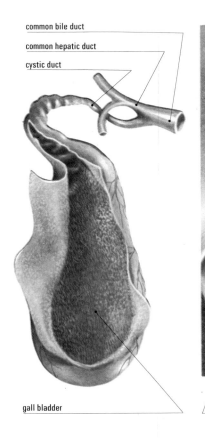

common bile duct

common hepatic duct

cystic duct

gall bladder

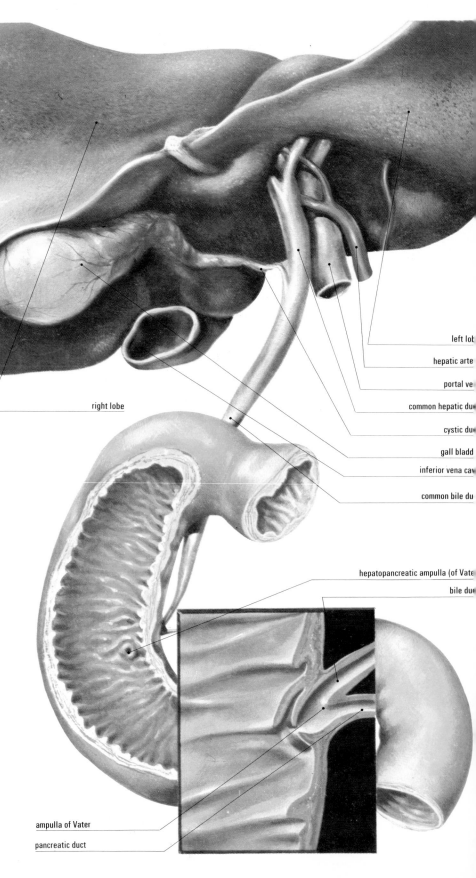

right lobe

left lob

hepatic arte

portal ve

common hepatic du

cystic du

gall bladd

inferior vena ca

common bile du

hepatopancreatic ampulla (of Vate

bile du

ampulla of Vater

pancreatic duct

Bile is a dark green fluid containing bile pigments (produced from the breakdown of hemoglobin, bile acids and salts, cholesterol and mucin. Passing radially in the intralobular canaliculi (in the opposite direction to blood flow) it is collected by the intrahepatic ducts which together form the right and left hepatic ducts. These then unite as the common hepatic duct which, when joined by the cystic duct from the gall bladder, becomes the common bile duct (right); linked in the head of the pancreas with the pancreatic duct (facing page, lower picture), the two ducts open into the second part of the duodenum through the ampulla of Vater (diagram enlargement, below right). Bile salts emulsify fat and therefore assist in the absorption of dietary fat and fat-soluble vitamins. Bile also constitutes an important exit pathway for certain drugs and poisons. Some 500 ml of bile is excreted every day; the gall bladder concentrates this volume and also acts as a reservoir, regulating the pressure within the biliary tree.

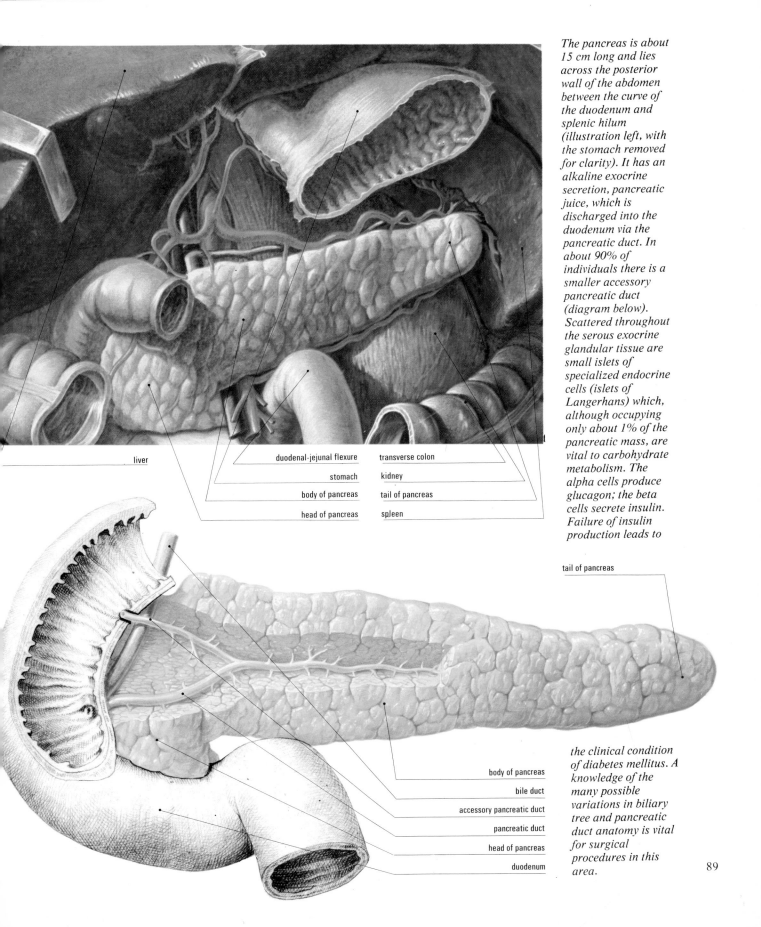

The pancreas is about 15 cm long and lies across the posterior wall of the abdomen between the curve of the duodenum and splenic hilum (illustration left, with the stomach removed for clarity). It has an alkaline exocrine secretion, pancreatic juice, which is discharged into the duodenum via the pancreatic duct. In about 90% of individuals there is a smaller accessory pancreatic duct (diagram below). Scattered throughout the serous exocrine glandular tissue are small islets of specialized endocrine cells (islets of Langerhans) which, although occupying only about 1% of the pancreatic mass, are vital to carbohydrate metabolism. The alpha cells produce glucagon; the beta cells secrete insulin. Failure of insulin production leads to the clinical condition of diabetes mellitus. A knowledge of the many possible variations in biliary tree and pancreatic duct anatomy is vital for surgical procedures in this area.

liver

duodenal-jejunal flexure

stomach

body of pancreas

head of pancreas

transverse colon

kidney

tail of pancreas

spleen

tail of pancreas

body of pancreas

bile duct

accessory pancreatic duct

pancreatic duct

head of pancreas

duodenum

89

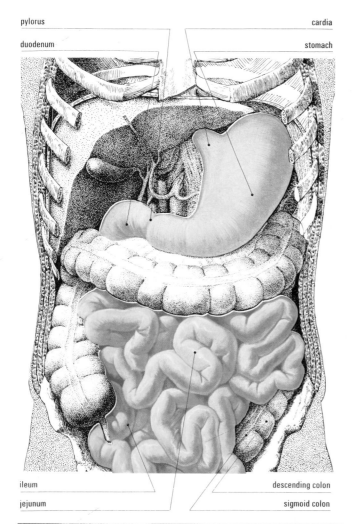

pylorus

cardia

duodenum

stomach

ileum

descending colon

jejunum

sigmoid colon

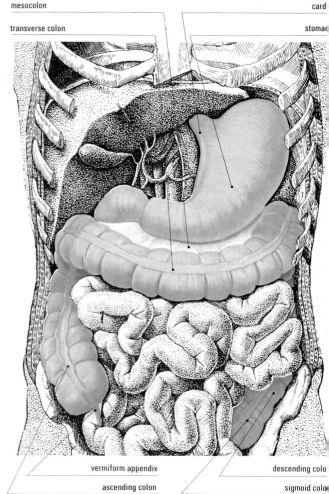

mesocolon

card

transverse colon

stoma

vermiform appendix

descending colo

ascending colon

sigmoid colo

The intestine can be simply summarized as a tube of varying caliber and flexible structure. It is divided conventionally into two parts: (i) the small intestine (diagram above left) which extends from the pyloric valve to the ileocecal junction and (ii) the large intestine (above right) which runs from the ileocecal junction to the anus. The small intestine, some 6 to 7 meters long, begins with 25 cm of duodenum. This curves around the head of the pancreas and is devoid of a mesentery. The duodenal mucous membrane is thrown into crescent-shaped folds (endoscopic view, lower left) which project into the bowel lumen to retard the progress of chyme as well as offering an increased area for absorption. The duodenum runs on into the jejunum and ileum; jejunum is slightly thicker and has a more complicated mucosal structure than ileum. It also has a slightly greater diameter (4 cm vs. 3.5 cm) but both are enveloped in layers of peritoneal mesentery, in which they hang in coiled loops from a linear attachment along the posterior abdominal wall. The blood supply of the jejunum and ileum is derived from branches of the superior mesenteric artery. These major vessels form anastomotic arterial arcades within the mesentery, from which straight arteries run to the gut wall. The jejunal wall is the more vascular.

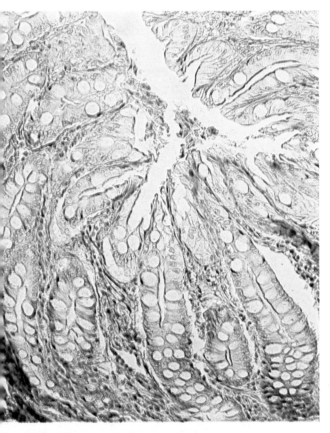

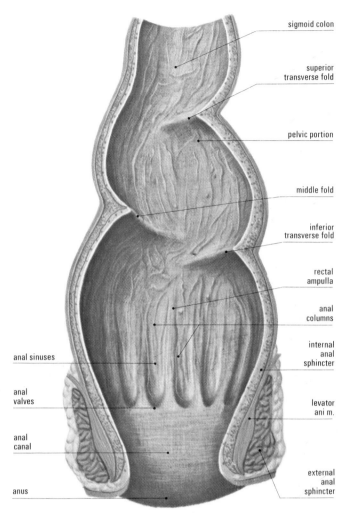

sigmoid colon

superior transverse fold

pelvic portion

middle fold

inferior transverse fold

rectal ampulla

anal columns

internal anal sphincter

levator ani m.

external anal sphincter

anal sinuses

anal valves

anal canal

anus

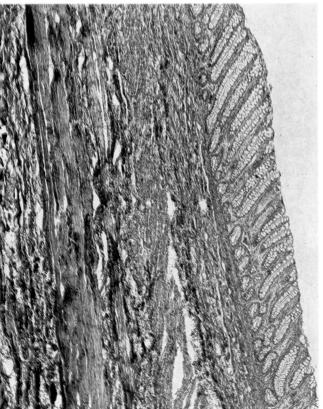

The large intestine is of greater caliber than its predecessor, but of shorter length — some 1.5 meters. Unlike the small intestine, it is relatively fixed in position. The outer longitudinal muscle fibers are modified into three bands (tenia coli) which cause the colonic wall to become puckered into haustrations. Commencing from the cecum, the ascending colon becomes transverse at the right colic (hepatic) flexure, then turns downwards into descending colon at the left colic (splenic) flexure. Passing into the lesser pelvis this forms a curving loop, the sigmoid colon, before dilating into rectum and anal canal (above). Some 3 cm from the ileocecal valve lies the base of the vermiform appendix. Of variable length and position, this blind-ended narrow tube is rich in lymphoid tissue. Although frequently the site of obstruction and inflammation, the diagnosis of acute appendicitis can be very difficult to make preoperatively because of these variations. The mucous membrane of the colon is pale and smooth while that of the rectum is darker, thicker and more vascular. A high power microphotograph (upper left) shows colonic epithelium to be glandular with mucus secreting goblet cells scattered amongst absorptive columnar cells. A lower power view (below left) shows this tubular arrangement more clearly.

91

Swallowing (deglutition) is a complex process involving the co-ordinated response of many different palatal and pharyngeal structures. The diagrams (below) show four phases in the swallowing sequence. Well chewed, and mixed thoroughly with saliva (upper left), the bolus lies on the tongue. In the initial voluntary phase, the tongue pushes upwards (lower left), against the hard palate, which channels the bolus posteriorly into the pharynx to begin the second, involuntary phase. The soft palate is tensioned and elevated against the pharyngeal wall to prevent nasal regurgitation. The larynx is also drawn up, beneath the hyoid bone (upper right) and closed off. Helped by gravity and spreading contraction waves in the superior, middle and inferior pharyngeal constrictor muscles, the bolus slips over the epiglottis (lower right) to gain access to the upper esophagus. The laryngeal movements in this rapid, complicated and vital process can be confirmed by placing a finger tip on the 'Adam's apple' during the act of swallowing.

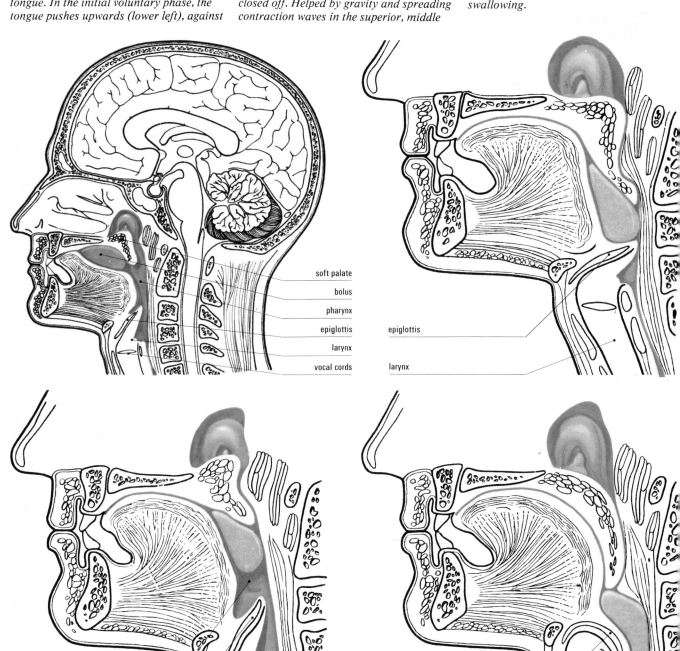

soft palate
bolus
pharynx
epiglottis
larynx
vocal cords

epiglottis

larynx

pharynx

epiglottis

larynx

epiglottis

larynx

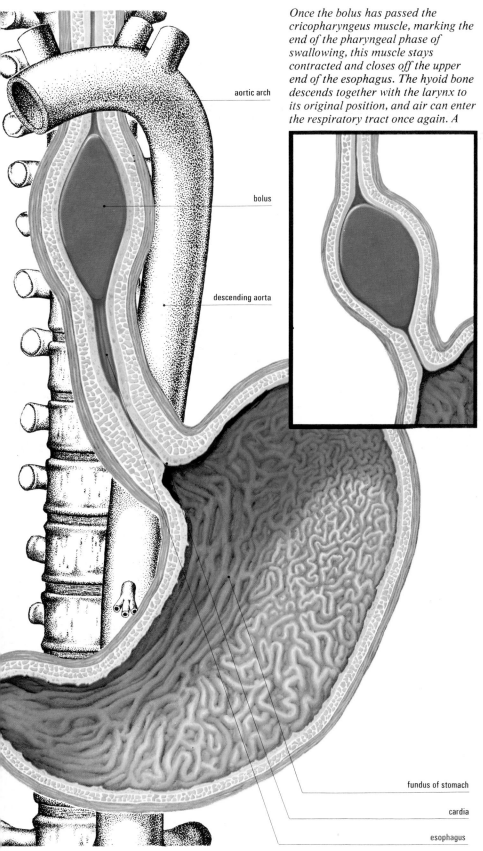

Once the bolus has passed the cricopharyngeus muscle, marking the end of the pharyngeal phase of swallowing, this muscle stays contracted and closes off the upper end of the esophagus. The hyoid bone descends together with the larynx to its original position, and air can enter the respiratory tract once again. A peristaltic wave begins which propels the bolus down to the stomach until it reaches the gastro-esophageal (cardiac) 'sphincter'. There is a slight delay at this point, with deformation of the bolus demonstrable in X-ray studies, until the 'sphincter' suddenly relaxes and the bolus passes into the stomach.

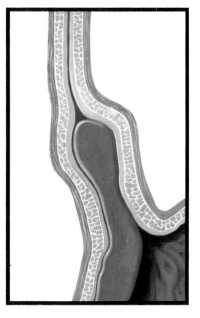

aortic arch

bolus

descending aorta

fundus of stomach

cardia

esophagus

Gastric tone also decreases to ensure that there is no sudden increase in intragastric pressure. This might otherwise cause regurgitation and vomiting. The cardiac 'sphincter' also contracts again to prevent reflux of acid stomach contents which can damage the unprotected esophageal mucous membrane. Other features that are important in this respect are the diaphragmatic crura which can pinch off the lower end of the esophagus during deep inspiration, and the actual angle formed between the esophagus and stomach is also critical. Occasionally these features are deficient, and a portion of stomach can pass upwards into the thorax, a condition termed hiatus hernia. The nervous control of swallowing is complex. Perfect timing at successive levels is required for smooth passage of the bolus. The voluntary phase is initiated by a precentral area of the cerebral cortex, but this has numerous connections with a medullary swallowing center, itself closely related to the nuclei of the vagus nerve.

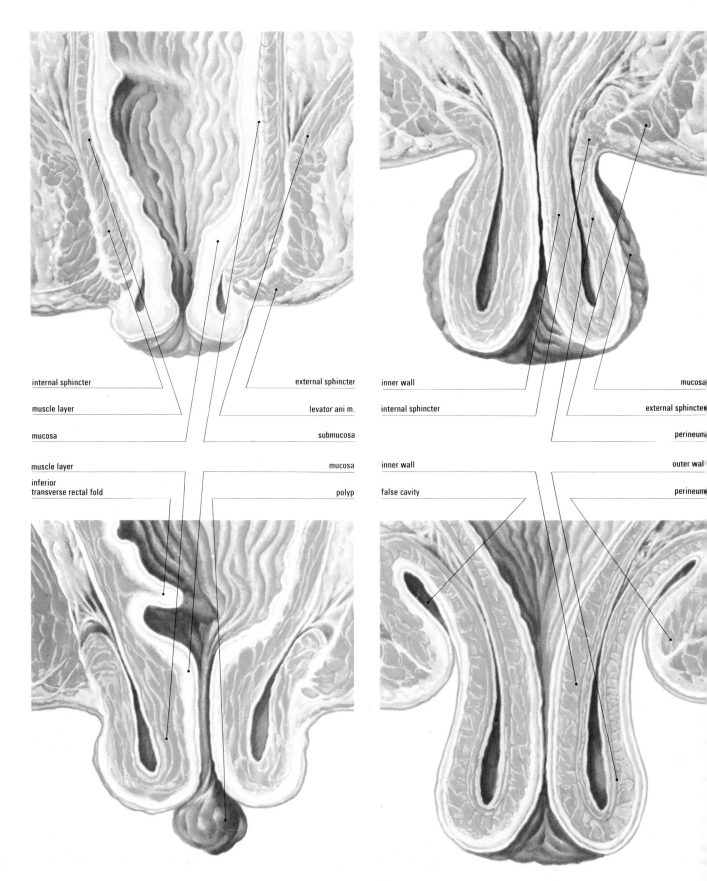

internal sphincter

muscle layer

mucosa

muscle layer

inferior
transverse rectal fold

external sphincter

levator ani m.

submucosa

mucosa

polyp

inner wall

internal sphincter

inner wall

false cavity

mucosa

external sphincter

perineum

outer wall

perineum

Prolapse of the rectum can take several different forms which, although appearing similar externally, must be accurately identified before treatment can commence. By definition, rectal prolapse occurs when the bowel wall descends through the anus in all parts of its circumference. If only mucosa and submucosa prolapse, sliding down over the muscular layer beneath, the prolapse is partial (illustration facing page, upper left). Partial prolapse rarely proceeds more than 5 cm beyond the perineal skin. Complete prolapse, or rectal procidentia, incorporates the muscle layers as well; this process of extrusion may involve a polyp at the apex (lower left) or else include a weak external anal sphincter (upper right) which undergoes inversion. In yet another variation (lower right) the sphincters are lax, but in their normal position. Rectal prolapse may occur in children or adults, but is especially common in patients with psychotic disorders who are long term residents of mental institutions. The cause is obscure. Poor tone in the pelvic floor musculature (especially the levatores ani) is usually blamed, along with laxity of the anal sphincters.

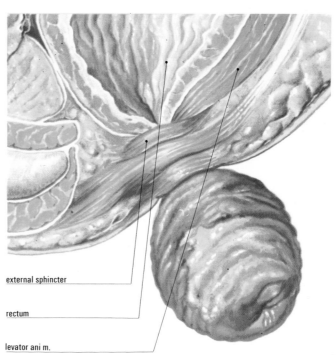

external sphincter

rectum

levator ani m.

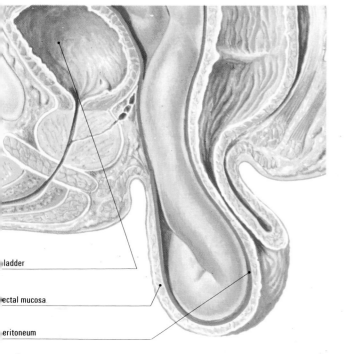

ladder

ectal mucosa

eritoneum

A deep rectovaginal or rectovesical pouch of peritoneum is also suggested as a predisposing factor for rectal prolapse, because a pouch of this kind may form a hernial sac containing a loop of small intestine (left) which pushes on the anterior wall of the rectum and encourages its descent. Note how in this case the anal orifice projects posteriorly due to the disparity in size of the prolapsed rectal walls. Incontinence of feces is obviously a major problem; strangulation (above) may also develop, with a reduction in the blood supply caused by spasm of the anal sphincters. The lining mucosa has turned a dusky red; in certain areas avascular necrosis has taken place, with secondary infection and the discharge of a purulent serous fluid. Treatment usually requires surgery. After the contents are returned to the abdomen, any hernial sac is identified and excised. The external sphincter may be strengthened by a silver wire suture, or else the redundant bowel loop is amputated and the cut edges sutured together.

Fiberoptic endoscopy has revolutionized the specialty of gastroenterology. Intestinal function and behaviour may now be inspected in vivo, both in health and disease, without recourse to indirect methods such as radiology. The basic features of the instrument were described on p. 8, but sophisticated and specialized versions have been developed for certain regions. A gastric ulcer (right) can be inspected, irrigated, photographed, biopsied and, if bleeding, treated by laser or diathermy coagulation. In addition, most endoscopic procedures can be carried out under local anesthetic and light sedation. As well as minimizing patient risk, this also reduces demand for hospital beds.

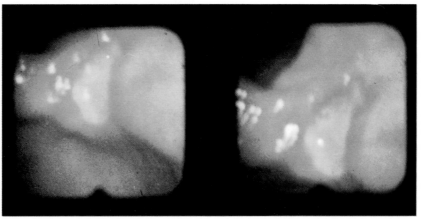

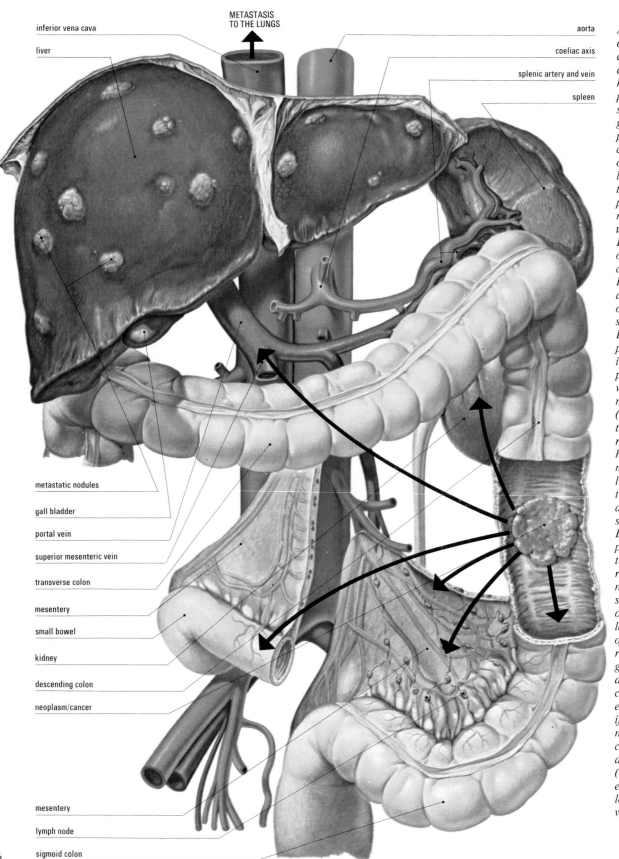

METASTASIS
TO THE LUNGS

inferior vena cava

liver

aorta

coeliac axis

splenic artery and vein

spleen

metastatic nodules

gall bladder

portal vein

superior mesenteric vein

transverse colon

mesentery

small bowel

kidney

descending colon

neoplasm/cancer

mesentery

lymph node

sigmoid colon

*A malignant grow
of the descending
colon can take
different forms and
has several potenti
pathways for
spreading along. T
growth may be
polypoid; annular,
causing stenosis an
obstruction of the
large bowel, or (as
the illustration, lef
plaque-like with a
rolled edge and
ulcerating center
Distant implantati
of cancer cells is
called metastasis.
How soon this occr
depends on the type
of cancer and its
speed of growth.
Early invasion of
pericolic veins resu
in clumps of cells
passing to the liver
where they form
metastatic nodules
(left). These can gr
to great size, almos
replacing normal
hepatic tissue. Som
metastases reach t
lungs and kidneys
the bloodstream, a
also produce
secondary growths
Lymphatic
penetration procee
to involvement of th
regional lymph
nodes, and direct
seeding can occur t
other parts of the
large bowel. The a
of surgery is to
remove the primary
growth completely
and restore bowel
continuity by end-t
end anastomosis or
if technically
necessary, the
creation of an
artificial anus
(colostomy). With
early surgery, the
long term results a
very good.*

the urogenital system

The urogenital system has two vital functions: the kidneys maintain the composition and volume of body fluids within very narrow limits, while the sex organs facilitate perpetuation of the species through the mechanism of reproduction. As a result of evolution the urinary and genital tracts have become completely different, except for the male urethra which is the final pathway for both urine and spermatozoa. This linking in description is therefore more traditional than functional. The basic unit of the kidney is the nephron. There are some two million nephrons in the paired kidneys which, with the ureters, bladder and urethra, constitute the urinary system. Homeostasis, the preservation of the body's internal environment in a physiological state, is largely due to the kidney's actions. Regulation of the water and electrolyte content, maintenance of a normal acid/base equilibrium, elimination of metabolic waste products and retention of vital substances are all features displayed by healthy kidneys. To achieve this remarkable range of functions, the kidneys are highly vascular organs, receiving one quarter of the cardiac output, approximately 1.3 liters per minute. From this large volume and the capillary/glomerular pressure difference which acts like a hydrostatic filtration pump, the kidneys elaborate about 170 liters of filtrate per day. As the urine passes through the different portions of the tubule, it is modified according to body needs by selective reabsorption and secretion. Eventually, only about one per cent of the original volume is passed down the ureters to the bladder reservoir, to await voiding by micturition. The male and female reproductive glands, the testis and ovary, have already been described in detail (pp. 48–49). Within the seminiferous tubules of the testis, spermatogenesis takes place. The spermatozoa pass via the epididymis to the vas deferens, a long tube leading to the seminal vesicles. In the female, the ova are discharged into the peritoneal cavity from ripened follicles.

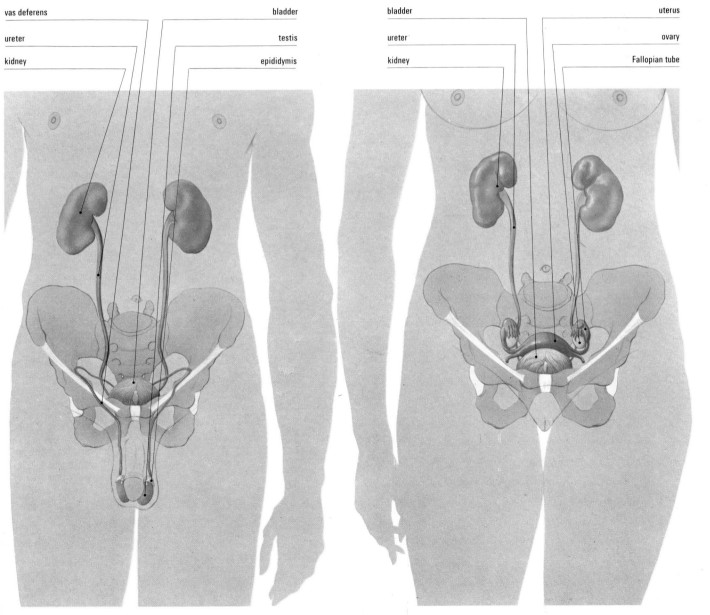

vas deferens   bladder   bladder   uterus

ureter   testis   ureter   ovary

kidney   epididymis   kidney   Fallopian tube

The two kidneys are retroperitoneal structures located on the posterior abdominal wall (below); surrounded by fatty connective tissue, they weigh between 130 and 150 gm each in the adult. Their close proximity to the vertebral column and abdominal aorta is well shown in the CAT scan (right). The basic renal structure (facing page, upper left) consists of an outer cortex and inner medulla, the cortex in turn covered by a thin fibrous capsule that is easily stripped off. Projecting from the hilum of each kidney, the renal pelvis is funnel-shaped and formed from the caliceal system; it is continuous with the ureter, a 30 cm long muscular tube which conveys urine by peristaltic contraction waves down towards the bladder. Section through the renal substance displays a number of medullary pyramids, their apices projecting into the calices and bases capped by a layer of cortex. Under the microscope (illustration facing page, upper right) these can be seen to consist of a large number of tortuous, densely packed uriniferous tubules. Studded throughout the cortex, a large number of Malphigian corpuscles are visible to the naked eye. Each corpuscle has two components: a dilated portion of the uriniferous tubule called the glomerular (Bowman's) capsule

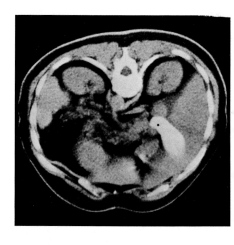

forms a thin sac closely applied to a capillary tuft, the glomerulus, derived from the renal arteriolar network. The proximal part of the uriniferous tubule also lies in the cortex and is highly convoluted; this leads on to a thinner-walled section which dips down into the medulla, forming the loop of Henle, before ascending again to become the distal convoluted tubule. From here, straighter junctional tubules drain into the collecting tubules and thence into the minor and major calices. A transverse section through the male pelvis (facing page, lower right) is also shown beside a detailed enlargement of the bladder neck, prostate gland and seminal vesicles.

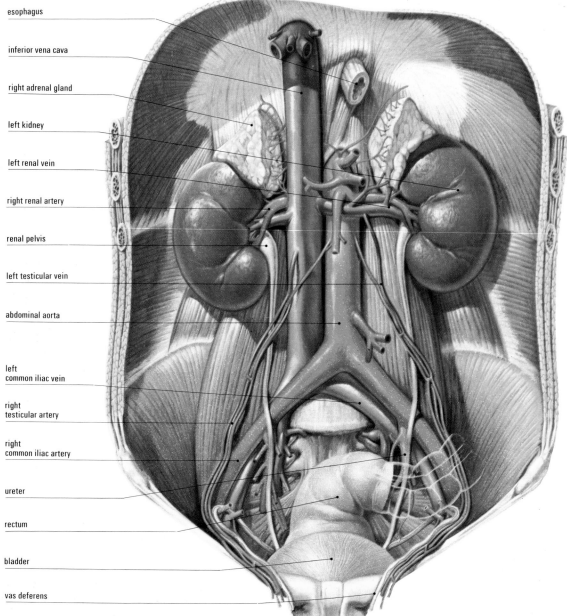

esophagus

inferior vena cava

right adrenal gland

left kidney

left renal vein

right renal artery

renal pelvis

left testicular vein

abdominal aorta

left common iliac vein

right testicular artery

right common iliac artery

ureter

rectum

bladder

vas deferens

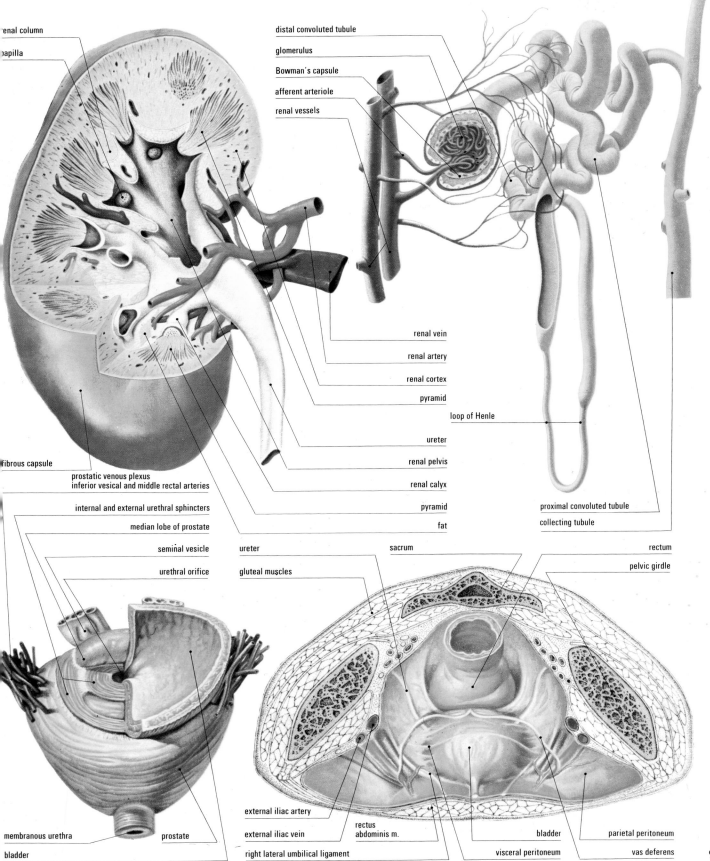

renal column

papilla

distal convoluted tubule

glomerulus

Bowman's capsule

afferent arteriole

renal vessels

renal vein

renal artery

renal cortex

pyramid

loop of Henle

ureter

renal pelvis

renal calyx

pyramid

fat

proximal convoluted tubule

collecting tubule

fibrous capsule

prostatic venous plexus
inferior vesical and middle rectal arteries

internal and external urethral sphincters

median lobe of prostate

seminal vesicle

urethral orifice

ureter

gluteal muscles

sacrum

rectum

pelvic girdle

external iliac artery

external iliac vein

right lateral umbilical ligament

rectus
abdominis m.

bladder

visceral peritoneum

parietal peritoneum

vas deferens

membranous urethra

bladder

prostate

99

The penis (below) is the male organ of copulation; it consists mainly of spongy erectile tissue, grouped into two corpora cavernosa and a single corpus spongiosum which ensheaths the urethra from the bulb to the glans. These are covered by a tough fibrous layer, a loose superficial fascia, and a thin outer layer of richly innervated skin. Erection occurs under parasympathetic control; rapid filling of the spongy tissues by blood compresses their draining veins so that the penis becomes stiff, facilitating its insertion into the vagina. Orgasm and ejaculation are mediated via sympathetic pathways. The terminal portion of the vas deferens and the ducts of the seminal vesicles form the ejaculatory ducts (right). The secretion of the seminal vesicles is alkaline and rich in fructose (p. 48) which provides energy for swimming spermatozoa. At ejaculation, rhythmic contraction of smooth muscle fibers in the vesicles and ejaculatory ducts pulse the seminal fluid down the urethra to the upper vagina.

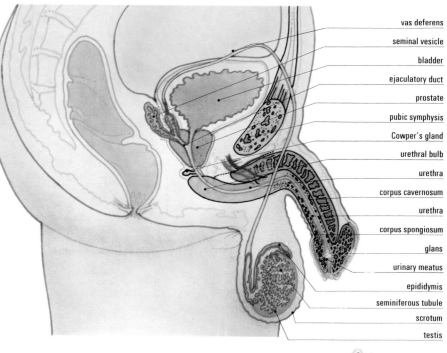

vas deferens
seminal vesicle
bladder
ejaculatory duct
prostate
pubic symphysis
Cowper's gland
urethral bulb
urethra
corpus cavernosum
urethra
corpus spongiosum
glans
urinary meatus
epididymis
seminiferous tubule
scrotum
testis

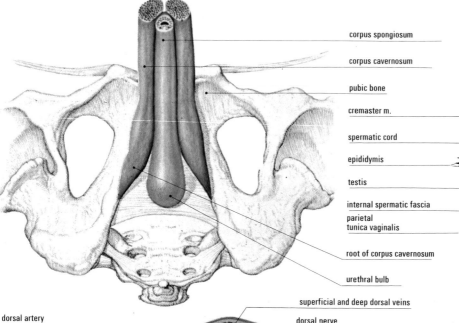

corpus spongiosum
corpus cavernosum
pubic bone
cremaster m.
spermatic cord
epididymis
testis
internal spermatic fascia
parietal tunica vaginalis
root of corpus cavernosum
urethral bulb

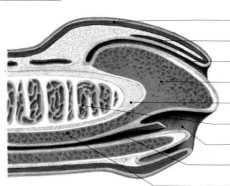

dartos
prepuce
preputial sulcus
glans
septum of penis
corpus cavernosum
urinary meatus
urethra
corpus spongiosum

superficial and deep dorsal veins
dorsal nerve

dorsal artery
connective tissue
penile fascia
corpus cavernosum
deep penile artery
urethra
tunica albuginea
dartos m.
bulbo-urethral artery

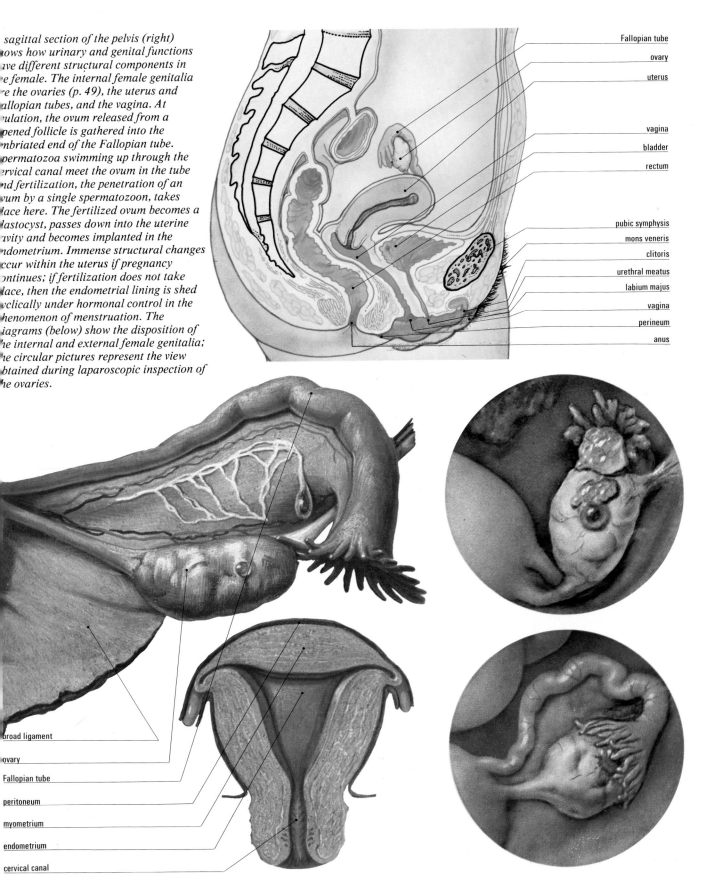

sagittal section of the pelvis (right)
ows how urinary and genital functions
ve different structural components in
e female. The internal female genitalia
re the ovaries (p. 49), the uterus and
allopian tubes, and the vagina. At
ulation, the ovum released from a
pened follicle is gathered into the
mbriated end of the Fallopian tube.
permatozoa swimming up through the
ervical canal meet the ovum in the tube
nd fertilization, the penetration of an
um by a single spermatozoon, takes
ace here. The fertilized ovum becomes a
lastocyst, passes down into the uterine
avity and becomes implanted in the
ndometrium. Immense structural changes
ccur within the uterus if pregnancy
ontinues; if fertilization does not take
lace, then the endometrial lining is shed
yclically under hormonal control in the
henomenon of menstruation. The
iagrams (below) show the disposition of
he internal and external female genitalia;
he circular pictures represent the view
btained during laparoscopic inspection of
he ovaries.

Fallopian tube
ovary
uterus

vagina
bladder
rectum

pubic symphysis
mons veneris
clitoris
urethral meatus
labium majus
vagina
perineum
anus

broad ligament
ovary
Fallopian tube
peritoneum
myometrium
endometrium
cervical canal

Glomerular filtration produces a fluid which is isotonic with plasma but contains very little protein or fat. During passage through the proximal convoluted tubule (below) many ions and small molecules are reabsorbed. The concentrations of sodium and chloride ions in the renal medulla are kept high by an active transport system; the loop of Henle passes into and out of this region to ensure a high rate of tubular water resorption. This regional osmotic factor also operates on the lining cells of the collecting tubules, but in addition these cells are affected by antidiuretic hormone (ADH) secreted by the posterior pituitary which alters their permeability to water. The glomerulus may be severely affected (microphotograph, right) by membranous deposits in certain conditions, leading to high blood pressure and possible renal failure.

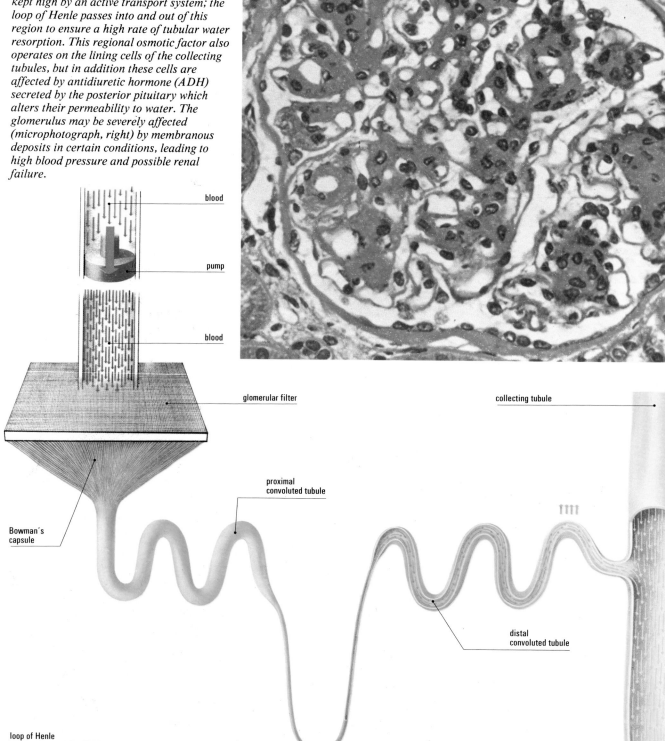

blood

pump

blood

glomerular filter

collecting tubule

Bowman's capsule

proximal convoluted tubule

distal convoluted tubule

loop of Henle

Index

ACKNOWLEDGEMENTS

For the collaboration offered in finding the
pictures contained in this atlas, we wish
to thank the following Institutes:
Centro Scoliosi Gaetano Pini di Milano
Neuroradiologia Nord, Milano
Clinica Chirurgica 2 del Policlinico, Milano
Clinica Dermatologica, Milano
Chirurgia plastica del Centro Ustioni di Niguarda, Milano
Istituto dei tumori, radiologia, Milano.

PHOTO CREDITS

page 1-3-14-24-40-44-59-74: AGA Italia Srl, Div. infrarossi, Milano
page 1-4-5-22-23-45-60-87: SELO, Sesto San Giovanni
page 4-16: Foto C. Bevilacqua, Milano
page 6: Nuclear Enterprises, Milano
page 6-7: Grazia Neri
page 7-20-34-46-54-64-77-86-98: EMI Medical Ltd, Slough, England
page 8: Istituto di Farmacologia dell'Università di Milano
page 9: Prof. E.G. Rondanelli
page 14-15-17-72-82-84-91: Enrico Giovenzana, Milano
page 16: Foto Dott. Pellegris, Milano
page 77: Ente Ospedaliero, Ospedale San Carlo Borromeo, Milano